Holiday Fun
Activity Book

Bob "Captain Kangaroo" Keeshan

illustrated by Vicki Redenbaugh

Fairview Press
Minneapolis, Minnesota

Library of Congress Cataloging-in-Publication Data

Keeshan, Robert.
     Holiday fun activity book / Bob "Captain Kangaroo" Keeshan ;
  illustrated by Vicki Redenbaugh.
         p.   cm.
     ISBN 0–925190–78–0 (pbk. : acid-free paper)
     1. Family recreation—United States. 2. Holidays—United States. 3.
Amusements—United States. I. Redenbaugh, Vicki Jo. II. Title.
GV182.8.K446   1995
790.1'91 — dc20   95–21548
                                                          CIP
                                                          AC

Activity research and design by Cindy Nelson.
Cover art and interior illustrations by Vicki Redenbaugh.
Cover design and page layout and composition by Circus Design.

First Printing: September 1995
Printed in the United States of America

99 98 97 96 95   7 6 5 4 3 2 1

For a current catalog of Fairview Press titles,
please call this Toll-Free number: 1–800–544–8207

Contents

Contents

Contents

July

August

September

October

November

December

An Introduction for Grown-ups
by Bob Keeshan,
TV's "Captain Kangaroo"

The title, *Holiday Fun Activity Book* may seem redundant because when we think of "holiday" we usually think in terms of fun, rejoicing and being with family. Therefore, in some ways, holidays contribute to building and strengthening families, especially now when so many of us are busy in activities outside the home. Today, most parents need to work; it is an economic necessity. This is certainly true in most single-parent households; almost fifty percent of American young children live in such a family structure.

Family is the basic unit of any society, and most nurturing of children—particularly before adolescence—takes place in a family setting. This is why warm parenting patterns are so vital to the successful nurturing of each of our children. Easier said than done! Parents are very busy these days, distracted from nurturing by the compelling drive to provide for the economic needs of family and children and often distracted by the many other intrusions of "modern technology" from movies and computers to video games and the accessibility of recreational activities. Where does this leave today's children? Often, they

are pushed down the priority totem pole by the numerous distractions of the modern lifestyle.

Kids don't grow well in such a sparse nurturing soil. *They* have not changed, although society and the structure of family have changed. They still need the same nurturing they needed forty years ago, four hundred years ago, probably even in ancient Greece! They need to know they are loved, to be shown they are loved, not merely to be told they are loved. They need access to a nurturing parent, as a spouse needs access to a spouse. They are little different in their needs from spouses and other adults. Try coming home some evening to your spouse who wants conversation—access to update the experiences of a busy day—try saying to that spouse, "Honey, I'm tired, go watch television." It doesn't work with a spouse and it doesn't work with a child, no matter how young. When you fail to spend time with your spouse a message is sent and received; when you fail to spend time with a child the same message is sent and received.

This does not mean you must spend a huge amount of time with a child. Most children want space of their own and may find too much together time oppressive. But spending enough time with a child, giving him or her access at regular times daily, will send a clear message to the child that you care enough to make yourself available. The message to the child is clear: "The most important person in my world—my parent—spends time with me, therefore, I must be of value." This goes a long way in building the self-esteem of a child and is the appropriate exercise of what I call, "parent power."

Most parents do not realize the enormous power they have to influence a child. Remember the old saying, "Do as I say, not as I do?" It has no place in a healthy parent-child relationship. Kids are much too smart. Everything you do, every behavior you model is picked up by an observant child (and most children are very observant). So use that natural parent power to influence a child in a very positive manner. The family setting is the principal place where parent and child come together and the place where the child is influenced by the behavior of the parent. That is one reason holidays are such an important part of family life.

There are holidays and there are holidays. The major days: New Year's Day,

Memorial Day, the Fourth Day of July, Labor Day, Thanksgiving, and Christmas are observed in the United States; most parents take a day off from the workplace, perhaps several days. Life around the home may be more relaxed and people seem to have more time for each other and the things that count—love, warmth in relationships, relatives not seen every day, and just plain good feelings.

Other days talked about in this book are not so universally observed. Some of them, like the twelve birthdays, one for each month, are personal but very important and exciting to the birthday child! Others have their origins in religious events and occasions. Some, like Backwards Day, International Book Day, Tuba Day, Grandparents' Day, Child Health Day, Sandwich Day, and National Flashlight Day are really observances more than holidays in the strictest sense, some for a purpose, some for pure fun. Counting birthdays, almost seventy holidays are represented in this book, enough to bring out the celebratory spirit in any family.

About those holidays that are religious in orientation: Represented are Christian, Jewish, Muslim, and Far-Eastern Religions. It is not my place to instruct a young child in any religion, that is a parental privilege, but we are, as the founders of this nation provided, a pluralistic society. We have often been referred to as a "melting pot," a "mosaic," a harmonious mix of peoples of varying ethnic and religious backgrounds. It is important for each child to appreciate their own "roots" and important to be sensitive to the background of other peoples. It is in this context that the religious-based holidays are important to the parent in nurturing a child to be sensitive to the many different people sharing this nation. It is a very American notion and tradition; it is a great strength of this nation. The religious holidays in this book observe the more universal aspects of those holidays. The intent is to teach a child the joys and customs of others sharing in our rich American heritage.

You may notice that frequent mention is made of visiting the local library as a source for a richer understanding of some observances and the use of books such as encyclopedias, to serve the same purpose. These are practices which, once acquired, will serve a child through a lifetime. Use the *Holiday Fun Activity Book* to have fun with games and projects on any day and to enrich a child through the conversation that can be skillfully woven by an adult during these activities.

As I mentioned in the introduction to this book's predecessor, *The Family Fun Activity Book*, it is important for an adult to remember the joys of childhood, to cast aside our very serious grown-up inhibitions, and to appreciate the joys of being a child on a great voyage of discovery. The child grows, not by passive activities such as television viewing, but by real life experiences—those experiences shared with an important adult and especially those experiences shared with a parent. It is the appropriate use of this "parent power" that fosters self-esteem and other developmental growth in a child. Spending time with a child should be fun. If it becomes a chore you have somehow missed the point.

Holiday and fun are indeed redundant, so enjoy the redundancy of fun on holidays. Remember the Thanksgivings you may have spent with Mister Moose and Mister Green Jeans at the table, Bunny Rabbit with a feast of roast carrots, and Mister Moose with a turkey stuffed with ping pong balls. Remember the great parade we always had on the Fourth Day of July, the snowman we built at Christmas, and the joy when we wished a "happy birthday to every one born in this month," and blew out the candles to mark the occasion. Those were good days and the joy and fun associated with them are in the pages of this book. Put it on your nurturing shelf and pull it down when you have some time to share some joy in the most important job you have in your life—parenting!

Holiday Fun

January

Activity Book

January Birthday

One the most popular features on "Captain Kangaroo" was the birthday party we held on the first weekday show of every month. We will celebrate a birthday every month in this activity book and each party will have the makings for decorations and activities keyed to that month's theme.

The theme for the first birthday—the January Birthday—is wintertime. Even if you live in a sunny and warm climate you can have fun with the snow and games and icy ice cream of a winter party. Use the age guidelines to choose the right activities for the right age and have yourself some fun in the snow!

Snowman invitations and party decorations

What You'll Need:

- white and black construction paper
- plain white paper
- white lunch bags
- markers
- glue
- plain standard size envelopes
- felt scraps (any color)
- cotton balls
- scissors
- tape

Here's How to Make Them:

1. Invitations: Cut white construction paper into 3" x 6" rectangles. (You can get six from one piece of paper.) Draw a snowman shape on one side of each piece. Cut hats for the snowmen from black paper and glue them on. Cut scarves from felt and glue them on, too. Draw on eyes, nose, and mouth for each. On the back write your invitation. Then put them in envelopes and send them to your friends.

2. Decorations: Cut snowflakes from plain paper and tape them around your party room. (If you want more elaborate snowflakes, see the directions for making glitter snowflake ornaments on page 276.) Tape some to your tablecloth too.

3. Party bags: Let guests glue cotton balls to white lunch bags to make a snowman. Cut out eyes, nose, mouth, and hats from construction paper and glue on. (Simply give them markers and let them draw winter designs on the bags, if you want an easier and less messy activity!) Fill the bags with candy or other small treats to take home.

Snowman cake and ice cream snowballs

What You'll Need

- ➤ two 9" round cake pans
- ➤ board, tray, or sturdy cardboard at least 12" x 20"
- ➤ aluminum foil
- ➤ cake mix
- ➤ vanilla cream or fluffy frosting

- ➤ fruit roll-up candy or fruit jerky
- ➤ gum drops
- ➤ vanilla ice cream
- ➤ coconut
- ➤ ice cream scoop

Here's How to Make Them:

1. Snowman cake: With a grown-up's help, follow the instructions on the cake mix for baking a two-layer cake. Carefully remove the layers from the pans. When the layers have cooled completely, cut a straight edge along one side of each. (You don't have to take much off.) Spread frosting along the flat edge on one piece. Transfer the cake to a foil covered board, putting the flat edges together to make a snowman shape. Frost the remaining sides and top of the cake. Cut a piece of fruit roll-up to fit across the neck. Cut two more pieces about 4" long. Make small cuts at one end of each to resemble a fringe. Arrange the pieces on the snowman to make a scarf. Add gumdrops for eyes, nose, mouth, and buttons. (Or substitute birthday candles!)

2. Ice cream snowballs: Scoop round, tightly packed balls of vanilla ice cream. Roll them in coconut. (Store them in your freezer until you are ready to serve them.)

More Party Fun:

Entertain your guests with these party games and activities. Choose which ones to play, depending on the ages of your guests.

● Freeze! (Ages 3-5) — Instruct the children to jump, skip, hop on one foot, touch their toes, or move around the room. Tell them to freeze in the middle of an action. They must hold their pose until you say "Unfreeze." Take turns being the leader. You can play this as an elimination game, if you want. Anyone who moves before you say, "Unfreeze," is out.

● Roll the snowman (Ages 3-5) — Set up two chairs about four feet apart. Take turns rolling a beach ball (or snowman) around the chairs. See who can go the fastest! (With older kids, form teams and play against one another.)

● Snowball race (Ages 6-7) — Give each person a spoon and six cotton balls. Have the players line up on one side of the room, across from a row of paper cups. At the starting signal, scoop up one cotton ball at a time and race across the room to drop it in your cup. If you drop a cotton ball midway you have to scoop it up and go back to the starting line. No hands may touch the balls—only the spoons. The first person to "shovel" all six snowballs wins.

● Winter wrap relay (Ages 6-7 and 8-10) — Gather two sets of winter outer garments: large boots, hats, mittens, scarves, jackets. Divide into two equal teams. (Enlist the help of grown-ups if you have an uneven number of people!) Have each team form a line. Put a pile of clothes at one end of each line. At the starting signal, the first person in each line quickly dresses in the clothes, then undresses and passes the clothes on to the next one in line. Continue on down the line. The first team to finish, wins. (To make the game more challenging, allow players to use only one hand while dressing and undressing!)

● Blizzard (Ages 6-7 and 8-10) — Before the party, cut several sheets of white paper in little pieces. Set up an electric fan on a table, and lay a sheet on the floor near the table. Give each player a paper cup and tell them they must remain on the sheet. (Make sure they are a safe distance from the fan.) At the count of three, turn the fan on high. Throw handfuls of paper into the air in front of the fan. Players catch the "snow" as fast as they can and put it in their cups. The one with the most snow wins. (This game can get a little messy, so have a vacuum cleaner handy!)

● Outdoor fun (All ages) — If you live in a cold climate, spend most of the party outside in the snow! Lie on your back and make angels. Build snow sculptures. Invite your guests to bring their skates or skis or sleds and hold a mini winter Olympics. You can even award medals. (See page 258 for directions on making medals from frozen juice can lids.)

New Year's Day

(January 1)

New Year's Day is a day for new beginnings. Start off your year by planning what you and your family hope to accomplish. What can you do to strengthen your family's ties? The following family calendar activity will help get you started for the new year! Get everyone in the family involved. Older kids can help create the calendar pages and younger kids can draw the pictures.

Make a family calendar
(All ages)

What You'll Need:

- ➤ 12 pieces of plain paper
- ➤ old magazines
- ➤ markers or crayons
- ➤ pen
- ➤ paper punch
- ➤ yarn

- ➤ snapshots of family members
- ➤ last year's calendar
- ➤ ruler
- ➤ transparent tape
- ➤ scissors
- ➤ glue

Here's How to Make It:

1. Draw a grid on one side of each piece of paper. Use a ruler to make your lines straight. Each grid should have five boxes going down and seven boxes going across.

2. Print the names of the months and days of the week at the top of the grids. Look to see on what day last year ended to figure out on what day the new year begins. Add numbers to the grids, starting each new month where the last one left off. Determine which months have 30 days and which have 31 by looking at last year's calendar, and remember that February has only 28 (or 29 in leap years)!

3. Run a strip of transparent tape across the top edge of each page to reinforce it. Then punch three holes evenly spaced across the top. Turn the pages over so that the holes are at the bottom of the page, and on the backside, draw a picture to go with the next month. (The back of January is February's picture, and so forth. On the back of December, draw a picture for January.) Tie the pages together loosely with yarn. Be sure to get the months in the correct order.

4. Mark holidays and special events throughout the year by gluing on pictures cut from magazines or family snapshots or by coloring in designs. Start planning family events for the coming months now!

More Family Fun:

● Families with school-age kids can look back over last year's calendar and recall the special events that took place. Invite family members to say what day each thought was the best day of the year. Give reasons for choosing that day.

● For families with young children, cut your old calendar pictures into a few pieces and use them as puzzles. Cut them into more pieces for older children. Challenge family members to see who can assemble them the quickest.

● School-age kids can play a math game with a calendar. Lay a calendar page at your feet, and take turns dropping three buttons onto the page. Add up the numbers on which the buttons land. The person with the highest score wins. (If adding three numbers is too difficult, use only two buttons, or let players use a calculator.)

Three Kings' Day
(January 6)

This day is the twelfth day after Christmas and commemorates the visit of the Magi, the three kings, to the infant. In some places it is celebrated as "Little Christmas," and is celebrated by Spanish speaking people in many countries.

In Puerto Rico, for instance, children set up tall, colorful figures of the three kings.

Make some kings to display in your house

(Ages 3-5 and 6-7)

What You'll Need:

- three empty, clean 1 quart bleach bottles
- cloth scraps
- foil gift wrap
- aluminum foil
- permanent black marker
- yarn
- scissors
- glue

Here's How to Make Them:

1. Cut cloth scraps into three 6" x 12" rectangles. (You will want three different colors or patterns.) Glue the cloth pieces around the bottom three-fourths of each bleach bottle.

2. Cut the foil gift wrap into three 12" squares. Fold each square into a triangle and wrap it around the neck of the bottle as a cape. Overlap the ends of the triangle and glue them together.

3. Glue yarn around the top of the bottle for hair. Draw on a face with the marker and glue on yarn for beards, if you want.

4. Cut a crown for each king from aluminum foil and glue it around the cap of the bottle. Then set your kings where people will notice them!

More Family Fun:

● In Mexico on the night before Three Kings' Day, children leave their shoes on the doorstep or window ledge for the Three Kings. They also leave a bowl of water for the camels to drink. In the morning, the water is gone, and their shoes are filled with treats. Why not try this custom with your family?

● With a grown-up's help, bake a Kings' Cake in the shape of a ring or crown. When it is cooled, decorate the cake with candied cherries and pineapple to make it look "jeweled."

Martin Luther King Day

(January 15)

Children are born free of any sense of discrimination. These negative concepts are "learned" from observation of adults and authority figures, often in their childhood. This holiday, commemorating the birthday of a great leader who represented a yearning to bring out the best in people, is an apt occasion for parents to use positive reinforcement to present this message to children. The reality is that we must live these principals for our children to model not just on this day but on every day of the year.

Play the Civil Rights "Match-Up" game

(Ages 6-7 and 8-10)

What You'll Need:

➤ 3" x 5" index cards or pieces of poster board
➤ marking pen
➤ encyclopedia or book on Martin Luther King, Jr., or the
Civil Rights Movement

Here's How to Do It:

1. Print each of the following people or events from the life of Martin Luther King, Jr. on index cards. *Make two sets* of cards. To help nonreaders play, draw simple pictures to accompany the words:

- Rosa Parks (African-American woman)
- The Montgomery Bus Boycott (bus)
- Southern Baptist Minister (cross)
- The Letter from the Birmingham Jail (window with bars)
- The March from Selma to Montgomery (footprints)
- The March on Washington (Washington Monument)
- Dr. King's "I Have a Dream" Speech (African-American child and white child)

- The Voting Rights Act of 1965 (ballot box)
- The Nobel Peace Prize (medal)
- "We Shall Overcome" (music notes)

2. Before playing the game, use an encyclopedia or a book about Martin Luther King, Jr. to research the history of the Civil Rights Movement in the United States. You can find books on the subject at your local library. Find out the significance of the events or people on the cards.

3. Shuffle both sets of cards together and lay them face down in a large rectangle on the floor or a table.

4. Let the youngest player go first. Take turns turning over two cards. If they match, keep the cards and turn over two more. A turn lasts as long as you can keep matching cards. If the cards don't match, turn them face down again, and let the next person have a turn. The person with the most matches wins.

5. To make the game more challenging for older children, allow players to continue only if they can name the significance of the cards they have matched. If they are unable to say how the event or person on the card fits into the history of the Civil Rights Movement, they may keep the cards, but play must pass on to the next player.

More Family Fun:

● Attend special events honoring Dr. Martin Luther King, Jr. that are held in your community. Check your newspaper or at your schools, churches, and local government offices for information about programs and events.

● Read together Dr. King's "I Have a Dream" speech. Draw pictures or write down your personal dreams of what you would like to see happen in our country. How can you work to make your dream and Dr. King's dream a reality?

Chinese New Year

The Chinese New Year is based on the lunar calendar and, therefore, falls on a day different from the New Year's celebration of Western nations. The Chinese celebration will fall between January 19th and February 19th. Find out when the day falls this year. It is a two-week festival and ends on Yu'an Hsiao, the Lantern Festival in which children parade with lanterns. Talk to children about the ancient Chinese culture, a civilization far older than civilizations to which many other Americans trace their roots. Talk about the contribution made by Chinese-Americans to the culture of this new land. Teach children to respect the customs and culture of this ancient civilization.

Make a Chinese lion puppet! (All ages)

What You'll Need:

- ➤ cardboard box large enough to fit over your upper body
- ➤ cardboard scraps
- ➤ old sheet
- ➤ paint
- ➤ masking tape or duct tape
- ➤ crepe paper streamers
- ➤ scissors
- ➤ glue

Here's How to Make It:

1. Cut off the flaps from the two sides of the box. Leave the front and back flaps on. Round the edges of the front flap to use as the lion's tongue. Cut a mouth opening above the flap, being careful to leave the flap on the box. Cut ears from the cardboard scraps and tape them to the head.

2. Paint features on your lion's head. Make them colorful!

3. Cut a four-feet wide strip from the old sheet. Paint colorful designs on the sheet. When it is dry, attach it to the back flap on the box for the lion's tail.

4. Glue or tape on crepe paper streamers to the lion's head and tail.

5. Put the box over your head and look out through the mouth hole. Invite all family members to climb under the tail, and dance through your house. Gung Hay Fat Choy! Happy New Year!

Make Chinese lanterns

(Ages 3-5 and 6-7)

What You'll Need:

➤ construction paper
➤ ruler
➤ stapler
➤ streamers (optional)

➤ scissors
➤ paper punch
➤ yarn
➤ yardstick or dowel

Here's How to Make It:

1. Fold a piece of construction paper in half, lengthwise.

2. Starting at the folded edge, cut 12 slits, 3-1/2" long.

3. Open the paper and staple the short sides together to form a cylinder. Punch a hole on either side of the top of the lantern and string yarn through for a hanger. Staple streamers to the bottom, if you wish, and attach the hanger to a yardstick or dowel for carrying the lantern in your lion parade.

More Family Fun:

● Eat a traditional Chinese meal to celebrate the new year. Make sure you have lots of rice!

● Red is the traditional color for Chinese New Year. Decorate your house with red streamers. In China, children receive "lucky envelopes" — little red envelopes with money in them!

● Glue a wide craft stick to the back of a paper plate to make a Chinese fan. Draw or paint flowers on it.

● A Chinese legend says that each year is ruled by one of twelve animals. Look below to find what animal rules this year. Draw a picture of it.

1996	Rat	1997	Ox
1998	Tiger	1999	Rabbit
2000	Dragon	2001	Snake
2002	Horse	2003	Sheep
2004	Monkey	2005	Chicken
2006	Dog	2007	Pig
2008	Rat		

National Handwriting Day

(January 23)

S how off your best penmanship today!

Personally designed stationery

(Ages 6-7 and 8-10)

What You'll Need:

> ➤ plain paper
> ➤ watercolor paints
> ➤ paint brush
> ➤ glue stick

> ➤ plain envelopes
> ➤ scissors
> ➤ newspapers

Here's How to Do It:

1. Spread newspaper over your table to protect it.

2. Use a paintbrush to wet the plain paper completely. Let it sit for five minutes and then wet it again.

3. Dip the paintbrush into the watercolor paint. Twirl and swirl it around on the paper. Repeat with other colors. If you get too much paint on, blot it with a paper towel. You can use the towel to add texture, too.

4. Let the paper dry. If it curls when dry, press it under a heavy book.

5. Cut the dried paper into strips or designs, and glue them onto a plain piece of paper to make stationery. You can also glue a triangle to the inside of the envelope flap to make a matching set.

6. Use your best handwriting to write a letter to a friend or relative on your personal stationery. A young child can draw a picture on the paper.

More Family Fun:

● Really practice your handwriting today by conversing with notes, not voices! Leave notes for family members in surprising places.

● Young children can practice "writing" in shaving cream on a kitchen countertop or other nonporous surface. (It cleans as they play!)

● Write fan letters to famous people. To find out where to send them, contact television stations, publishers, and other agencies. Your local librarian may be able to help.

● Write a letter to someone you admire from history. Tell about your life and how it is different from back then. How is it the same?

Backwards Day
(Last Friday in January)

Children delight in doing silly things but they can also learn from such antics as those of Backwards Day. Here are some suggestions for you but I'll bet you and your child can think of dozens of additional backwards activities. See just how silly you can get. Unwind and lose your inhibitions to really enjoy this one!

Turn your day around!
(All ages)

What You'll Need:

➤ a fun-loving attitude!

Here's How to Do It:

1. Start your morning with your favorite supper meal and eat under the table, not on it! Be sure to finish the day with breakfast. Or eat your meals backwards — begin with dessert! Yum!

2. Wear your clothes backwards or inside out.

3. Try to do as much as you can backwards. Play board games from finish to start. Walk backwards around the block (but be careful). Tell a story from end to beginning or try singing a song backwards. Have fun! Tomorrow is back to normal!

More Family Fun:

● Backwards Day originated in a school in Indiana. For more information on the holiday, contact Unity Lutheran School, 5401 South Calhoun, Fort Wayne, IN 46807.

● Look backwards! Spend some time looking back on your family's life together. Browse through photo albums (back to front, of course), talk about accomplishments, and enjoy reminiscing!

February

Activity Book

February Birthday

Although the 12 birthday parties are placed at the beginning of each month they are intended to be celebrated on any day of the month or any day of the year, for that matter. If you particularly like this pirate theme, or any of the other themes, use them any day, any month. The only rule is to have fun!

Ship's Ahoy! Sail off on this birthday adventure, but watch out for the pirates!

Treasure map invitations and pirate party decorations

What You'll Need:

- brown paper bags or brown wrapping paper
- markers or crayons
- standard-sized envelopes
- white paper tablecloth

- toothpicks
- plain white paper
- walnut shells
- clay
- scissors

Here's How to Make Them:

1. Invitations: Crumple up a paper bag or brown wrapping paper, then press it out flat. Tear the paper into irregular squares, to look like old parchment. Draw a ship in one corner and a dotted line around the outside of the paper that leads to an island with an X on it. Write, "This map leads to a birthday adventure!" on the map and add your party information. Make a map for each guest. Fold them up and put them in envelopes for mailing. If you want, draw a bottle outline on the back of the envelope. That way you're sending a message in a bottle!

2. Treasure map tablecloth: Turn a paper tablecloth into a big treasure map. Use crayons or markers to color on water, islands, ships—whatever! Include a "compass rose" in one corner.

3. Walnut ship party favors: Carefully split apart walnuts and pick out the nuts. Make sure you have one walnut shell half for each person. Press a marble-sized ball of clay into the bottom of each shell. Cut small paper sails for each. At the party, invite your guests to assemble their boats by sticking a toothpick through the paper sail and inserting it into the clay.

Treasure chest cake

What You'll Need:

- ➤ 9" x 13" cake pan
- ➤ large plate or tray
- ➤ table knife
- ➤ chocolate bar
- ➤ gem shaped fruit chews
- ➤ birthday candles

- ➤ cake mix
- ➤ serrated knife
- ➤ chocolate frosting
- ➤ red licorice twists
- ➤ foil-covered chocolate candy coins
- ➤ yellow coated chocolate candies (like M & Ms™)

Here's How to Make It:

1. With a grown-up's help, bake the cake, following the directions on the package for a 9" x 13" single layer. Carefully remove the cake from the pan and let it cool.

2. When it has cooled completely, cut the cake in half. Transfer one piece to a large plate. Frost the top. Place the second piece on top of the first. Use a serrated knife to round off the long edges on the top, so that the cake resembles a treasure chest.

3. Frost the sides and top of the cake with chocolate frosting. Smooth the frosting as well as you can. Use a table knife to make an indentation in the frost-  ing about two inches from the top, all around the cake. Break a chocolate bar into three pieces. Attach two horizontally to the back for hinges. Place the last piece on the front for a latch. Press yellow candies along the edges of the chest to represent brass rivets. Bend the red licorice twists and insert them in the sides of the chest as handles. Scatter foil-covered choco- late candy coins and gem-shaped fruit chews on the plate around the chest. Stick birthday candles in the top.

More Party Fun:

Sail off into fun with these party games and activities. Choose which ones to use, depending on the ages of your guests.

● Find buried treasure (Ages 3-5) — Fill a large tub with sand and set it on a plastic tablecloth (for easy clean up). Hide small prizes like little rubber balls or plastic figures or jewelry in the sand. (Make sure there is one per guest.) Let each player dig with a teaspoon to find the treasure. (No feeling with your hands is allowed!)

● Polly Parrot (Ages 3-5) — Parrot what Polly says or does! Let kids take turns being Polly. Everyone else must repeat Polly's words or actions. Who can be the funniest Polly?

● Pass the hats (Ages 6-7 and 8-10) — You need a cassette player or a radio and three pirate hats or sailor hats (or any hat) for this game. Form a circle. Place one hat on the head of the birthday person. Start the music and begin passing the hat around the circle, from head to head. Stop the music. The person with the hat is out. Add a second hat and start the music again. When the music stops, two people are out. Start again, this time with all three hats! Keep playing until all but one is eliminated.

● Treasure hunt (Ages 6-7 and 8-10) — Hide a bag of treats for everyone somewhere in your house. Write a series of clues on pieces of paper. Save out the first clue and hide the rest. (Make sure that each clue will correctly lead guests to the next one.) Give the first clue to the players and see how fast they can find the prize!

● Outdoor fun (All ages) — If you live where there is snow, work together to make an icy snow pirate. Or bury a treasure in the snow and give guests the honor of finding it. Let them dig with snow shovels—no maps allowed!

● Make pirate ships that really float! (All ages) — See page 210 for instructions on making ships from soap bars. If it's warm enough to set up a wading pool outside, race your ship against the others.

African American History Month
(February 1–28)

The enormous contribution made to American culture by African Americans is celebrated this month.

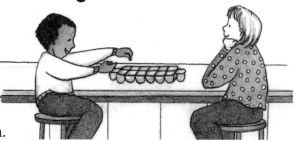

There far more contributions than have been noted here. This is an opportunity for parents to use reference works (from home or in the library) to make children aware of the contributions of African Americans to this land of ours. For older children there are many books which any librarian would be happy to refer to a parent or child. The vast continent of Africa contains many different cultures; this is reflected in the African counting game, Mankala. The matching game helps older children to identify many African Americans by name and contribution.

Play Mankala—an African counting game! (Ages 6-7 and 8-10)

Mankala is played in many parts of Africa. It is known by several different names. In East Africa they call it Mankala. In West Africa it is Oware or Ayo. In South Africa it is called Ohono.

What You'll Need:

- ➤ two egg cartons
- ➤ 48 dried beans
- ➤ tape
- ➤ two people

Here's How to Play:

1. To make a mankala board, cut the tops off both egg cartons. Cut two separate cups from one carton bottom and tape them to the ends of the other carton bottom.

2. Place four beans in each of the cups of the main egg carton. The two cups you attached are your banks, where you will keep the beans you win. (In East Africa, they use seeds or stones. They call it Hasa.)

3. Choose which player will go first. The first player always has the longest turn. He or she takes all the beans from any cup. Then, starting with the next cup on the left the player drops one bean at a time into each successive cup. After dropping the last bean into a cup, the player then takes all the beans from that cup and continues dropping one in each consecutive cup. The first player's turn ends when he or she drops the last bean into an empty cup.

4. The second player then chooses any cup and begins his or her turn exactly like the first player.

5. Whenever you drop your last bean in a cup that has only three beans in it, you get to keep all the beans in that cup. Put them in your bank. However, if you put a bean in a cup with three others, and it's not your last bean, the other player gets the beans in that cup.

6. The player who gets the next to the last four beans gets the rest of the beans in the carton. The person with the most beans at the end of the game, wins!

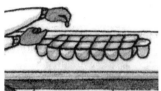

More Family Fun:

● Dig into history a little this month and find out more about these and other African Americans. Older kids and parents might play this matching game on pages 36–37. Who can match the most people with their accomplishments? (Answers are at the bottom of page 38.)

1.	Booker T. Washington	**A.**	Abolitionist and diplomat
2.	Thurgood Marshall	**B.**	Preacher and abolitionist; born Isabella Baumfree
3.	Marian Anderson	**C.**	Conductor on the Underground Railroad
4.	Frederick Douglass	**D.**	Opera singer and delegate to the United Nations
5.	Sojourner Truth	**E.**	Educator and first president of Tuskegee Institute
6.	Harriet Tubman	**F.**	Broke baseball's color barrier when he joined the Brooklyn Dodgers in 1947
7.	Jackie Robinson	**G.**	Ragtime pianist and composer
8.	Malcolm X	**H.**	Sprinter who won three gold medals at the 1960 Olympics
9.	Scott Joplin	**I.**	Fought at the Battle of Bunker Hill on June 17, 1775
10.	Peter Salem	**J.**	Performed one of the first two open-heart operations in the world
11.	Henry Blair	**K.**	First African-American Supreme Court Justice
12.	Hank Aaron	**L.**	Invented the corn-planter and cotton-planter
13.	Dr. Daniel Hale Williams	**M.**	Painter who is called the father of African-American art
14.	Aaron Douglas	**N.**	Home Run record holder

15. George Washington Carver   **O.** Leading spokesman for African-American Pride; founded the Organization for Afro-American Unity in 1963

16. Louis Armstrong   **P.** Won four gold medals at 1936 Olympics

17. Shirley Chisholm   **Q.** Botanist, chemist, and educator remembered for experiments with peanuts

18. Benjamin Banneker   **R.** Jazz trumpet player

19. Gwendolyn Brooks   **S.** First African American woman elected to the House of Representatives

20. Jesse Owens   **T.** Gospel singer

21. Mahalia Jackson   **U.** Member of Admiral Peary's expedition to the North Pole; placed U.S. flag at the Pole

22. Matthew A. Henson   **V.** Inventer, astronomer, and mathematician who helped to lay out Washington, D.C.

23. Martin Luther King, Jr.   **W.** Pulitzer Prize-winning poet

24. Wilma Ruldolph   **X.** Preacher, civil rights leader, and Nobel Peace Prize winner

25. Rosa Parks   **Y.** A college founder and president who gave advice to presidents Roosevelt and Truman

26. Mary McCleod Bethune   **Z.** Was arrested for not giving up a bus seat, which led to the Montgomery Bus Boycott in 1955

● Make a poster commemorating one of the people from the game above. Use an encyclopedia to learn more about the person you've chosen.

● Langston Hughes was an award-winning African-American poet and playwright. At the library, check out a book of his poems. Read them or have someone read them to you. Draw a picture of how one of his poems makes you feel. Try writing a poem of your own.

(Answers: 1-E; 2-K; 3-D; 4-A; 5-B; 6-C; 7-F; 8-O; 9-G; 10-I; 11-L; 12-N; 13-J; 14-M; 15-Q; 16-R; 17-S; 18-V; 19-W; 20-P; 21-T; 22-U; 23-X; 24-H, 25-Z, 26-Y)

Groundhog Day

(February 2)

What is a groundhog anyway? Most rural children and many living in the suburbs are familiar with this small animal, but many children, especially those who live in urban areas, have little knowledge of this cute little critter. Explain the myth about the groundhog leaving his winter home on this day to test for the arrival of spring. If he sees his shadow he retreats to the comforts of his burrow and the prediction is for six more weeks of winter. Ask your child whether he or she thinks there can be any proof to this story. The indoor garden allows us to make spring arrive when we want it, groundhog or not!

Play a musical game,"Pop Goes the Groundhog"

(Ages 3-5)

What You'll Need:

➤ at least two people

➤ a bath towel for each "groundhog"

Here's How to Play:

1. Crouch down and cover your head with a towel. Now you are a groundhog in your burrow.

2. Mom or dad or another player hide behind a chair and sing the following song to the tune of "Pop Goes the Weasel." They may choose to sing whichever ending they wish, so be ready! When you hear the word *pop*, jump up quickly and scurry around the room. But be ready to pop back into your hole, if the other player jumps out and you see your shadow!

> Deep inside his cozy, warm hole,
> the Groundhog sleeps all winter,
> until the morn of Feb'rary two...
> POP goes the Groundhog! (Pop up quickly!)

> *Choose either of the following verses:*

40

If the sky is cloudy and drear,
the Groundhog goes a-creeping.
He knows that Spring is finally here
No time for sleeping! (Stretch and run around the room.)

If the day is sunny and bright
The Groundhog sees his shadow.
It gives him such a terrible fright...
POP goes the Groundhog!
(Pop back in hole!)

3. Sing the song several times, choosing the ending you wish.

Head start garden

(Ages 6-7 and 8-10)

Did the Groundhog see his shadow? Are you tired of waiting for spring? Move the seasons along with this indoor garden idea!

What You'll Need

- empty plastic gallon or half-gallon milk container
- scissors
- acrylic craft paints
- paint brush

- spoon
- potting soil
- coarse sand
- flower or garden seeds

Here's How to Make It:

1. Have a grown-up cut away the front part of the carton as shown in the picture, leaving about two inches at the bottom to form the planter.

2. Paint spring designs like flowers and bugs around the opening. Paint a big yellow sun inside the container near the top.

3. Spoon a thin layer of sand into the bottom for drainage. Add $1^{1}/_{2}$ inches of potting soil.

4. Plant and water the seeds according to the directions on the seed package. Put your plant starter in a sunny window and be sure to keep the soil moist. When the seedlings are big enough, you can transplant them.

Shadow art (All ages)

Here's an activity for warmer climates. Show the Groundhog that shadows are nothing to fear! Create shadow outline pictures.

What You'll Need

- sidewalk chalk
- a sunny day
- at least two people

- smooth concrete surface (sidewalk or driveway)

Here's How to Do It:

1. Get permission from your parents to draw on the sidewalk or driveway. (Invite them to help!) And be careful to stay away from traffic.

2. Take turns outlining the shadows of each person with sidewalk chalk. Remember to stand still.

3. Draw on features and color on clothes. Sign your name by your masterpiece. And don't fuss when the rain washes it away!

More Family Fun:

● If you don't have a garden in which to plant your seedlings, plan on starting one when the weather is warm. If you don't have the space, plant the seedlings in a container garden for outside your door, or give them to someone who has a garden.

● Become "Spring Spies" and keep track of spring signs. Make a list of things to look for, such as when the last snow melts, the first robin or bug appears, the first spring flower blooms, or the tree in your yard leafs out. By each item leave a space for the name of the spy and the date he or she sees the spring sign. You may want to predict a date for each item. Check later to see if you were right!

● Do you live in an area where the seasons don't change too much? Pretend you are the Groundhog. If the day is cloudy, get dressed and venture out. But if the morning dawns sunny and bright, spend the day in your pajamas—unless you have to go somewhere!

Valentine's Day
(February 14)

This secular holiday originated as a religious commemoration of Saint Valentine. For many years, especially in English-speaking countries, it has been a day to send expressions of caring and love, and very often it is an occasion for fun and comic greetings. It's a great day to express our feelings for family members and friends, especially those we do not see every day, perhaps a grandparent, aunt, or uncle. Have as much fun as you can think of using your imagination, but do it with love.

Make valentines for the special people in your life! Here are some ideas!

Lace-up heart
(Ages 3-5 and 6-7)

What You'll Need

➤ poster board
➤ paper punch
➤ crayons or markers

➤ scissors
➤ tape
➤ yarn

Here's How to Make It:

1. Cut a six-inch heart from poster board. Punch holes around the outside edge.

2. Color designs on the heart. You can color on the front and back!

3. Wrap tape around the end of an 24" long piece of yarn. Lace the yarn through the holes in the heart, starting at the top. When you get back to the beginning, tie a bow.

4. Write the words (or have a grown-up do it), "You are SEW special!" on the heart. Sign your name or draw a picture and give the valentine to someone you love!

Hidden message valentines

(Ages 6-7 and 8-10)

What You'll Need:

➤ white construction
  paper
➤ white crayon
➤ scissors
➤ watercolor paints
➤ paint brush

Here's How to Make Them:

1. Cut large hearts from the construction paper.

2. Write messages on the hearts with white crayon and deliver them.

3. To read the message, brush watercolor paint over the hearts. Like magic the words will appear!

Valentine pop-up
(Ages 8-10)

What You'll Need:

> construction paper
> ruler
> glue

> pencil
> scissors
> markers

Here's How to Make It:

1. Cut the construction paper into two 6" x 6" squares.

2. Fold one square in half and draw half a heart shape on it. (The center of the heart is the fold.) Cut along your pencil line, but do not cut the heart out completely. Leave a small portion along one side uncut, so that the heart is still attached to the paper.

3. Unfold the paper and push the heart forward. Refold the paper.

4. Fold the second piece of paper in half and open it.

5. Spread glue on the back of the paper with the pop-up and carefully glue it to the inside of the second piece of paper, making sure the edges line up. (The heart should pop out.)

6. Cut additional small hearts from a different color of construction paper and glue them to the outside of your card. Add your message and deliver!

More Family Fun:

● Decorate Valentine mail bags for each family member and put them in a central location the week before Valentine's Day. Leave a pad of paper and a pencil close by, and encourage family members to leave a note or picture in somebody's bag each day. On Valentine's Day, drop the appropriate cards in each bag. Then let everyone dig through their bags and read their "mail."

● Hold a Valentine bake-off! Use your favorite recipe or buy refrigerated dough. Then gather cookie cutters, sprinkles, and canned frosting to make edible Valentines to share with friends!

Presidents' Day

(Third Monday in February)

George Washington, our first president, was born on February 22, 1732. Abraham Lincoln, the nation's sixteenth president, was born seventy-seven years later in 1809. Their birthdays were once celebrated separately in various states. Now, Presidents' Day is set aside nationally to celebrate the birthdays of both presidents. Take a moment to teach some of the things you know about these two presidents. How did their lives and actions affect the way we live in the United States today? Why is each of these presidents remembered today? Remember, the parent is the natural teacher for a child.

Tricorner hat and stovepipe hat (Ages 3-5)

Hats off in honor of George Washington and Abraham Lincoln!

What You'll Need:

➤ 12″ x 18″ black construction paper
➤ transparent tape
➤ scissors

Here's How to Make Them:

1. Have a grown-up help you cut a 12" diameter circle for each hat. Cut a circle out of the center of each large enough to fit your head. Save one cut out for later.

2. For the tricorner hat, simply fold up the edges of the circle to make a triangle.

3. For the stovepipe hat, roll a 9" x 12" piece of construction paper into a cylinder. Make it the size of the hole in the brim. Cut several 1" long slits in the bottom of the cylinder and insert it through the hat brim. Turn up the notched edge of the cylinder and tape it to the underside of the brim. Tape the circle you saved to the top of the cylinder.

Presidential Trivia (Ages 6-7 and 8-10)

What You'll Need:

➤ 3" x 5" index cards
➤ watch with a second hand

➤ pen or pencil

Here's How to Do It:

1. Write each of the following bits of trivia on separate index cards. Add any questions you can think of!

- Who does legend say threw a dollar across the Potomac River? (*George Washington*)
- Which president delivered the Gettysburg address? (*Lincoln*)
- Which president was good at building log cabins? (*Lincoln*)
- Whose face appears on a dollar bill? (*Washington*)
- Whose face appears on a five dollar bill? (*Lincoln*)
- George Washington is known as the father of what? (*Our country*)
- Who crossed the Delaware River at Christmas? (*Washington*)
- Who is remembered for freeing the slaves? (*Lincoln*)
- Where do George Washington and Abraham Lincoln appear together? (*On Mount Rushmore National Monument in the Black Hills of South Dakota*)
- Who does legend say could not tell a lie? (*Washington*)

- Where are the Washington Monument and the Lincoln Memorial located? (*In Washington, D.C.*)
- What was the name of George Washington's plantation? (*Mount Vernon*)
- On what U.S. coin does Lincoln's face appear? (*The penny*)
- Which president has both a city and a state named after him? (*Washington*)
- True or false? George Washington lived in the White House. (*False*)
- True or false? Abraham Lincoln was a general during the Civil War. (*False*)
- True or false? George Washington was president during the Revolutionary War. (*False*)
- What president is said to have chopped down a cherry tree? (*Washington*)
- Who had a beard, George Washington or Abraham Lincoln? (*Lincoln*)
- What was the name of George Washington's wife? (*Martha*)

2. To play, divide into two teams. Shuffle the cards and place them face down in a pile.

3. Teams take turns drawing a card and reading the question aloud. Give the opposing team 30 seconds to respond. If they answer correctly, they score a point. If they cannot answer within 30 seconds or if they answer incorrectly, the other team scores a point. The team with the most points wins.

More Family Fun

● Reenact famous moments from the lives of George Washington and Abraham Lincoln. Pretend to cross the freezing Delaware River with General Washington or listen to Lincoln deliver the Gettysburg Address. Remember to wear your presidential hats!

● Start off Presidents' Day with a special breakfast. Decorate your table with red, white, and blue. Cut French toast into strips and build a "log cabin" with the pieces. Pour cherry syrup over the top. Then share the stories of Lincoln splitting logs and Washington cutting down the cherry tree.

Id ul-Fitr
(End of Ramadan)

Ramadan is a month-long observance of great religious significance to followers of Islam. During Ramadan, Muslims get up before the sun rises each day and have breakfast and then do not eat or drink anything until after the sun sets. The month-long fast is broken on the first day after the new moon and is celebrated as Id ul-Fitr. Muslims often celebrate for two days following Ramadan. People give gifts of sugared almonds and other treats in decorated boxes to friends. Many Muslims send Id cards to each other with a special greeting written on them. In Turkey, Id ul-Fitr is known as "the candy holiday." Children get candy coins wrapped up in handkerchiefs. In Sudan, children receive candy dolls with beautiful paper fans.

Because all Muslim holidays follow the Islamic calendar, Ramadan can fall on any number of months. At present, it is being observed in February.

Create Islamic patterns
(Ages 6-7 and 8-10)

What You'll Need:

> construction paper
> glue

> scissors
> pencil

Here's How to Do It:

1. Islamic art is based on geometric patterns like circles, triangles, hexagons, squares, and rectangles. (Islamic religion does not allow making pictures of living things, so you will not find designs that include people or animals on Islamic clothing or architecture. Geometric patterns based on flowers and plants are acceptable.) Look around your house for geometrical shapes that you can trace to make your pattern. Cans or drinking glasses can be used to make circles. Small boxes or blocks can be used to make squares. A ruler will help you make a straight line.

2. Draw your shapes on different colors of construction paper and cut them out. Arrange them in patterns on another sheet of paper. When you are satisfied with the pattern, glue it to the paper.

More Family Fun:

● Use your pattern to make a bookmark or a card to give as a gift. Or design some place mats for your family's table tonight.

● Try making designs using different colors of building blocks like Legos or Duplos.

● For young children, cut out geometrical shapes and glue them to index cards. Make several cards for each shape. Let the kids arrange the cards to make a pattern. You can also use them as flash cards to learn shape names.

March

Activity Book

March Birthday

Calling all sleuths! You're invited to a mystery birthday party!

Invitations and party decorations

What You'll Need:

- 3″ x 5″ lined notepad
- pencil or pen
- envelopes
- ink pad

- construction paper
- scissors
- paper tablecloth
- plastic magnifying glasses or poster board and plastic wrap

Here's How to Make Them:

1. Invitations: Fold construction paper to make cards that fit the envelopes. For each invitation, write the following on a page of lined notepad:

CLUES:

1. Cake crumbs
2. Candles
3. People with mysterious packages

Tear out the notepad page and glue it to the front of the card. Write your party information inside. Mail the invitations to your friends.

2. Party table: Cover your table with a paper tablecloth. Press your fingers onto an ink pad and make fingerprints all over the paper tablecloth. Buy plastic magnifying glasses at a party goods store or discount store, or cut poster board into the shape of a magnifying glass and glue on plastic wrap to simulate glass. Put one by each guest's plate.

Sleuth cake

What You'll Need:

- ➤ cake mix
- ➤ round cake pans
- ➤ vanilla cream frosting

- ➤ chocolate gel icing in a tube
- ➤ birthday candles
- ➤ plastic magnifying glass

Here's How to Make It:

1. With a grown-up's help, follow the directions on the package for baking and assembling a two-layer cake. Frost the cake with vanilla cream frosting, making it as smooth as possible.

2. Lay a plastic magnifying glass across the top of the cake. Draw on fingerprints with chocolate gel icing. Put the prints all over the cake. Arrange the birthday candles around the edge of the cake top. (Only an adult should light the candles!)

More Party Fun:

Try your hand at solving a case with these games and activities. Choose which ones to use based on the ages of your gumshoe guests! (Note: In case you didn't know, a gumshoe is a detective.)

●   Pieces to the puzzle (Ages 3-5) — Before the party, take apart a puzzle and hide the pieces around the room. Tell guests that solving a mystery is like putting together a puzzle. You have to find the clues and see how they fit together! Hunt for the puzzle pieces. As you find them, try to assemble the puzzle.

●   Following a lead (Ages 3-5) — Before the party tie small prizes onto long pieces of yarn. Make one for each guest. String the yarn back and forth across the room, criss-crossing the different pieces. When guests arrive, have them each follow a different string to find their prize.

●   Describe the suspect (Ages 3-5 and 6-7) — Sit in a circle. The birthday person is the detective. The detective keeps his or her eyes open while everyone else closes theirs. Then the detective describes another person in the circle, but doesn't say the person's name. Everyone tries to guess who the suspect is. The first person to guess right becomes the next detective.

●   Memory game (Ages 6-7 and 8-10) — A good memory is important for a detective! Arrange a dozen or more different objects on a tray. Let everyone look at the tray for ten seconds. Then remove the tray from the room. Give the detectives paper and pencil and have them list as many things as they remember from the tray. The one who remembers the most is the winner.

● Missing evidence (Ages 6-7 and 8-10) — Lead guests to the scene of the crime (another room). Let them observe the room for a minute. Then usher them out. While everyone is out, remove one item from in the room. Call the guests back in. Let them guess what has disappeared. The first person to guess correctly gets to hide the next item.

● Dust for fingerprints (Ages 8-10) — Check for fingerprints on hard surfaces. Dust on cornstarch or graphite powder with a soft paint brush. (Graphite powder can be made by filing a pencil lead with a nail file). Use cornstarch on dark surfaces and graphite powder on light or clear surfaces. If you find a print, lift it off with a piece of transparent tape.

St. Patrick's Day

St. Patrick, who lived over 1500 years ago, is the patron saint of Ireland. Although it is a religious holiday in many places it has become the day to celebrate the Irish people and the contributions their small population made in places around the world. The principal color of Ireland is green and, thus, we have provided you with lots of green fun. The shamrock (a clover-like leaf) is also associated with Saint Patrick and Ireland and thus, the shamrock hunt. It is said that on Saint Patrick's Day everyone is Irish. So, happy Saint Patrick's Day to you!

Paint your day green! Celebrate with an all-green meal! (All ages)

What You'll Need:

- ➤ a variety of green foods your family enjoys
- ➤ green food coloring
- ➤ green construction paper
- ➤ white construction paper
- ➤ scissors
- ➤ gold or green glitte
- ➤ green crayon or marker
- ➤ glue

Here's How to Do It:

1. Involve everyone in the fun! Plan a menu using as many green foods as you can. (How many green foods can you name?) Here's one suggestion: spinach quiche (add green food coloring to the egg mixture) with tossed green salad (chopped lettuce, broccoli, celery, green onion, green pepper, and fresh peas), and lime gelatin. Top off the meal with chocolate mint ice cream or a frosty shamrock shake (mint milkshake)!

2. Make special place mats for each person in your family. Cut green construction paper shamrocks and glue them onto white paper. Add leprechaun "footprints" by sprinkling green or gold glitter over dots of glue, and write a "Good Luck" message on each place mat!

More Family Fun:

● Before your meal, go on a shamrock hunt! Young children will especially enjoy this activity. Cut shamrocks from paper and hide them around your house or yard. Cut out one four-leaf clover and hide it too. Give each player a paper bag and let them go! Award the players one hug for every shamrock found. Give the person who finds the four-leaf clover the seat of honor at your dinner table!

● Legend says that St. Patrick chased the snakes out of Ireland. Turn a pair of old socks into snake puppets and act out the story.

● Check your library for books about St. Patrick, the country of Ireland, or those wee folks called leprechauns. Spend time after dinner reading the stories aloud.

Mardi Gras

In New Orleans the last night before Lent begins is one big costume party! Celebrate Mardi Gras with all the trimmings!

Carnival mask

(All ages)

What You'll Need:

> paper plate

> scissors

> paper punch

> glue

> string or yarn

> markers, crayons, or paint

> construction paper

> dowel and masking tape (optional)

> assorted decorative items such as glitter, chenille sticks, cotton balls, foil, feathers, ribbons, or streamers (use what you have readily available!)

Here's How to Make It:

1. Cut the paper plate in half. Cut out holes for your eyes (a grown-up can help do this) and cut out a wedge shape so the mask will fit over your nose.

2. Now comes the fun part! Color or paint your mask the way you want it. (Purple, green, and gold are traditional Mardi Gras colors.) Then glue on all sorts of decorations. Make your mask as elaborate or as simple as you want! Use your imagination!

3. After the mask is decorated, punch a hole on each side and attach strings so it can be tied around your head. If you want your mask on a holder, eliminate the strings and tape a dowel to one side of the mask. (Paint the dowel or cover it with ribbon, if you wish.)

Trinket bags
(Ages 3-5)

Mardi Gras parades feature elaborately decorated floats and costumed people throwing beads and gold coins to the crowd. Here are some trinkets to create for yourself!

What You'll Need:

- ➤ string or yarn
- ➤ colored fruit cereal rings
- ➤ margarine tub lids or poster board
- ➤ juice glass
- ➤ foil
- ➤ pen
- ➤ crayons or markers
- ➤ stapler
- ➤ scissors
- ➤ paper lunch bags
- ➤ streamers

Here's How to Make Them:

1. Cut 24" lengths of string or yarn. Thread fruit cereal rings onto the yarn and tie the ends together to make an edible necklace!

2. Make doubloons (gold coins) by tracing around a juice glass onto the lids of margarine tubs or onto poster board. Let a grown-up cut out the circles. Then cover them with foil.

3. Don't forget to decorate a booty bag to carry your treasures! Staple streamers all around the top of a paper lunch bag to make it festive or draw on your favorite designs.

More Family Fun:

● Hold your own Mardi Gras parade! Locate a recording of some Dixieland jazz or zydeco music (check your local library), don your masks, wave streamers, march around, and toss your trinkets. Happy Mardi Gras!

● In England, they don't celebrate Mardi Gras, but they do observe Pancake Day on the last day before Lent begins. They eat lots of golden pancakes with fancy toppings, and some towns even sponsor pancake races! Have pancakes for all your meals today—wrap them around sausages, pile fruit on top, or just eat them with sticky syrup.

Easter

Easter is a very serious religious holiday. It is also a day of joy, and many Easter customs reflect that joy. Regardless of your religious beliefs, it is a day when these joyous practices can be a fun experience for all. Many different cultures are involved in the celebration of Easter and our activities reflect this diversity.

Have an egg-stra special celebration this year!

Easy-dye marble Easter eggs (Ages 3-5)

What You'll Need:

➤ Red, yellow, blue, and green liquid food coloring

➤ paper towels

➤ zipper-type sandwich bags

➤ hard-boiled eggs

➤ wet cloth

Here's How to Do It:

1. Let a grown-up fold a paper towel into quarters and slip it into a sandwich bag. Drip about 10 drops of food coloring between the layers of the paper towel and let it sit for about a minute. (You may mix colors.)

2. Wipe the egg with a wet cloth and then put it into the bag. Seal the bag, squeezing out the excess air.

3. Here's the kids' part: roll the bag around in your hands for a while, making sure the paper towel is squeezed against the egg.

4. Open the bag, and carefully take out the egg. Now you're ready to put in another egg. You can make several eggs with just one bag!

Build a castle egg-straodonaire! (Ages 6-7)

What You'll Need:

➤ cardboard tubes

➤ shoe box or other small box

➤ construction paper

➤ springtime gift wrap (optional)

➤ markers or paint

➤ scissors

➤ glue

➤ Easter grass

➤ decorated eggs

Here's How to Make It:

1. Cover the shoe box with construction paper or gift wrap or paint it a bright color. Cut the paper tubes into six-inch lengths for corner towers. Paint them or cover them with paper. Turn the box upside down and glue the towers to the four corners.

2. Cut windows and doors from construction paper and glue them to the box and towers. Or, you may want to paint them on. Use markers to decorate your castle any way you want.

3. Place the castle on your table and spread Easter grass around the outside. Arrange your eggs in the grass, but save the four

74

prettiest ones to place in the tops of your castle towers! If you have little Easter figurines, you can place them around your castle too!

Make cascarones
(Ages 8-10)

Spanish tradition says that getting one of these confetti-filled eggs smashed on your head brings good luck!

What You'll Need:

➤ empty eggshells
➤ markers
➤ paper punch
➤ glue

➤ scraps of colored paper
➤ tissue paper
➤ scissors
➤ funnel

Here's How to Make Them:

1. Carefully break a hole about the size of a nickel in the top of a raw egg. Pour out the contents and rinse out the egg with warm water. Let it dry.

2. Draw patterns on the empty eggshell with markers. Be careful not to drop the egg!

3. Make piles of confetti by cutting colored scraps of paper into tiny squares or punch out little circles with a paper punch. You don't need special paper; recycle your Sunday comics or old magazines or gift wrap.

4. Use a funnel to fill the egg with confetti. Then glue a round piece of tissue paper over the hole and let it dry.

5. You're ready! Smash your egg on someone's head for a fun-filled Easter surprise!

More Family Fun:

● Check out other egg decorating techniques. Some of the most intricately designed eggs have come from Ukraine, where the art has been handed down for generations. A good book for further reading is *Ukrainian Easter Eggs and How We Make Them* by Anne Kmit, Loretta L. Luciow, and Luba Perchyshyn (Minneapolis: Ukrainian Gift Shop, 1979).

● Hold an Easter egg hunt or an egg roll with your family, and invite your neighbors, too—the more people, the more fun!

Holiday Fun

April

Activity Book

April Birthday

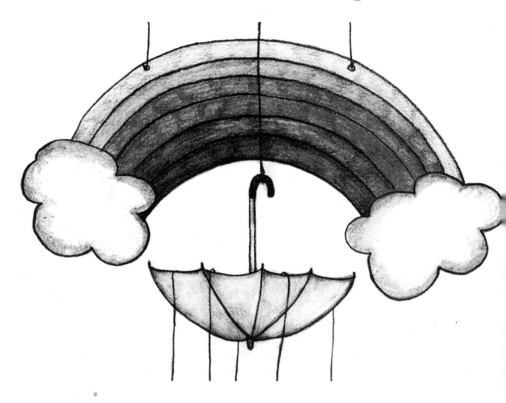

April showers may bring May flowers, but they also bring rainbows. Celebrate an April birthday with a rainbow party!

Hidden rainbow invitation and party decorations

What You'll Need:

- white and gray construction paper
- brass fasteners
- crepe paper streamers in rainbow colors
- poster board
- quilt batting or cotton balls
- fishing line or string
- markers
- stapler
- glue
- scissors
- paper punch
- tape or straight pins

Here's How to Make Them:

1. Invitation: Cut a semicircle from a quarter sheet of white construction paper. Color a rainbow on the semicircle. Cut two cloud shapes from gray construction paper. They should be large enough to completely cover the semicircle when put together. Attach the cloud shapes on each side of the rainbow with brass fasteners so they can be rotated to reveal the rainbow. Write

"What's behind the clouds?" on the cloud pieces. On the rainbow, write, "A Rainbow Party!' and add your party information.

2. Rainbow decoration: Make a rainbow to hang over your table. Cut a large rainbow shape from poster board. Staple on crepe paper streamers for each band of color. Do this on both sides of the rainbow shape. Cut two cloud shapes from posterboard and glue quilt batting or cotton balls to both sides. Staple the cloud pieces to the ends of the rainbow. Punch two holes along the top of the rainbow (to keep it straight) and hang it up with fishing line or string.

3. Rainbow table: Cover your table with a white tablecloth or white paper. Attach rainbow colors of crepe paper streamers to one end of the table (with pins or tape). Bring the streamers one at a time across the table, twisting each slightly.

Rainbow cake and ice cream

What You'll Need:

- ➤ cake mix
- ➤ vanilla cream frosting
- ➤ marshmallow creme
- ➤ plastic sandwich bags
- ➤ birthday candles
- ➤ round cake pans
- ➤ red, yellow, green, and blue food coloring
- ➤ Neapolitan brick ice cream

Here's How to Make It:

1. With a grown-up's help, follow the directions on the cake mix for baking a two-layer, round cake. Let the adult remove the layers from the pans and let them cool completely. Place one layer on a plate and spread marshmallow creme on top. Put on the second layer. Reserve about a cup of vanilla frosting. Tint the remainder a light blue color and frost the top and sides of the cake with it.

2. Spoon the remaining frosting into seven plastic sandwich bags. Add food coloring to each bag to make these colors: Red, orange, yellow, green, blue, and purple. (Orange is made by mixing one part red and two parts yellow; purple is one part blue and two parts red.) Squeeze the bags to mix the colors. Cut off a corner on each bag. Pipe a rainbow onto the top of the cake by squeezing on the bag. Add marshmallow creme clouds at the ends of the rainbow. Stick birthday candles in the clouds or in each color of the rainbow.

3. Cut Neapolitan ice cream (vanilla, chocolate, strawberry) into slices and top each with a piece of rainbow cake.

More Party Fun:

Entertain your guests with these party games and activities. Choose which ones to use, depending on the ages of your guests.

- Rain game (All ages) — This rain game won't get you all wet! Stand in a circle and let the birthday person be the leader. The leader starts by rubbing his or her hands together. The next person to the left joins in, then the next and the next, until everyone is rubbing their hands. Then the leader begins to snap fingers. The next person stops rubbing hands and begins snapping fingers. Everyone continues to rub hands until their turn to snap fingers. (If kids can't snap fingers, they may substitute light hand clapping.) Then leader begins to slap thighs. This motion is sent around the circle as before. When everyone is slapping thighs, the leader adds stomping feet, while continuing to slap thighs. When everyone is slapping thighs and stomping feet, reverse the activities, going backwards through the sounds that have been made. Continue until silence is passed from person to person as you stop rubbing your hands.

- Rainbow wands (Ages 3-5) — Let guests tape rainbow colored crepe paper streamers to paper tubes. Put on some music and wave them around!

- Rainbow step game (Ages 3-5) — Cut large circles from each of these colors of construction paper: red, yellow, orange, green, blue, and purple. (Cut as many circles from each color as there will be people at the party.) Tape the color dots to the floor in a big circle, alternating the colors. Have everyone begin on the same color. As you call out colors, the children step from dot to dot. Switch colors whenever you want. Start out slowly, then pick up the tempo!

● Pick a raindrop party favors (Ages 3-5 and 6-7) — Suspend an upside down umbrella and fill it with small prizes and treats. Attach one end of a piece of string to each favor and tape a small paper raindrop to the other end. Let the strings dangle down over the edge of the umbrella. Guests may pull on a raindrop to get their prize.

● Color scavenger hunt (Ages 6-7 and 8-10) — Give each person a paper bag and an old magazine. Tell players to tear out as many pictures as they find of these colors: red, orange, yellow, green, blue, and violet. Set a timer for one minute. Who found the most?

● Over the rainbow volleyball (Ages 6-7 and 8-10) — String rainbow colored streamers across the room or between two chairs. Play the game according to volleyball rules, but substitute a balloon for a volleyball. For a more animated game, play with three balloons, not one!

● Twister™ (Ages 6-7 and 8-10) — Play this game if you have it or borrow it from someone who does. It might make a good present for the birthday boy or girl to open first!

April Fool's Day
(April 1)

When I was a child this was one of our favorite "holidays." A classmate was certain to say, "Wow, look at that big stain on your tie." I'd look down and immediately be greeted by shouts of, "April Fool!" Boys rarely wear ties today but the innocent jokes of April Fool's Day are just as much fun. The key, of course, is to keep the jokes innocent and fun for all. This, by the way, is the end of this book. April Fool!

Play "Jester, Make Me Laugh" (Ages 3-5 and 6-7)

What You'll Need:

➤ at least three players (more is better!)

Here's How to Play:

1. Select one person to be the Jester. The remaining players are the royal court. Sit in a circle with the Jester in the middle.

2. The game is simple: the Jester does or says anything he or she wishes to make the royal court laugh. However, the Jester may not touch any member of the royal court. (Tickling is not allowed!) The royal court tries very hard not to laugh. The first person who laughs becomes the new Jester and the game begins again.

3. Play as long as you like or until your side ache from laughing!

The no-pop balloon challenge (Ages 8-10)

Stump your friends with this amazing trick!

What You'll Need:

➤ two balloons of different colors

➤ transparent tape

➤ a straight pin

Here's How to Do It:

1. Blow up both balloons. Place a piece of transparent tape on one of them. Do not let the other person see the tape.

2. Challenge someone to stick a pin through the side of a balloon without popping it. Give your friend the balloon *without* the tape on it. Then cover your ears—because it will pop when your friend tries!

3. Now use the second balloon to show how you can poke a pin through it without it popping. *The trick is to stick the pin through the tape.* The balloon may lose some air, but it will not pop!

4. Quickly clinch the trick by graciously allowing the other person to try again, but don't reveal the secret. Hold the balloon for your friend, keeping your finger over the tape to conceal it. Get ready for the bang! April Fool!

More Family Fun:

● Stick a riddle in each family member's lunch bag today. At supper, see who solved it. Here are some riddles to get you started. (The answers are on the next page—but don't look until you've guessed!

1. What two things can't be eaten for dinner?
2. For what vegetable do you throw away the outside, cook the inside, eat the outside, and throw away the middle?
3. Who wears a cap but has no head?
4. What get's wetter the more it dries?
5. What month has 26 days?
6. How much dirt is in a hole, two feet square?
7. What runs all day but doesn't go anywhere?
8. What's black and white and red all over?
9. What bow can't be tied?
10. Why did the porcupine cross the road?

● Tell jokes around the dinner table. Check out the joke book section at your library.

● Read aloud stories about famous fools, like Hans Christian Andersen's, *The Emperor's New Clothes.*

● At the library, check out the book, *Bet You Can't,* by Vicki Cobb and Kathy Darling (Avon Books, 1980), for other science impossibilities to fool your family and friends. The book also gives a scientific explanation for each trick.

Answers to riddles

1. Breakfast and lunch
2. Corn on the cob
3. A bottle
4. A towel
5. All the months

6. None—a hole is empty
7. A clock
8. A newspaper or a sunburned zebra
9. A rainbow
10. Because he was stuck to the chicken

International Children's Book Day

(April 2)

This is a nifty occasion for a parent to remember the importance of books and reading in any culture. The greatest role model for children is the parent, and if the parent reads, the child will want to read. In early years, reading to children is very important if a love of reading and books is to be fostered. Introduce your child to the library, borrow some books, and make a habit of reading on a regular basis. The books that you loved as a child are probably still

published and loved by today's children, and there are many newer books published since your childhood for you to discover and for your child to enjoy. If you have the resources, visit a good book store with your child and make a book selection or two, to build a library for the child. It will be one of the child's fondest possessions. Please don't force your child to read. Reading will come at different times to different children. It's called, "reading readiness," and placing pressure on a child to read earlier than they are ready is known to be counterproductive. Allow them to acquire a love of books and stories and reading skills will come to them at the appropriate time. An added note: young children can be rough on books. Try to teach a respect for books, a respect that will last a lifetime. I still remember the way my mother caressed a book when she handled it. Her respect for books has lasted for me to this day. I love books!

Bring your favorite book to life! (Ages 3-5 and 6-7)

What You'll Need:

➤ a favorite storybook
➤ costume materials, such as scarves, hats, and other old clothes
➤ an active imagination

Here's How to Do It:

1. As a family, settle down in a quiet, comfortable spot and read aloud your favorite book. Listen as if it were the first time you have heard the story. Pay close attention to the pictures. Pick out your favorite character.

2. When the story is finished, act it out! Assign parts, and gather all kinds of costumes. (They don't have to look just like the ones in the pictures!) Try to tell the story in your own words. If you want to change the ending, go ahead! Have fun!

Fractured fairy tales
(Ages 6-7 and 8-10)

What You'll Need:

➤ a collection of familiar fairy tales ➤ plain paper

➤ pencil ➤ a timer

➤ at least four people

Here's How to Do It:

1. Divide into two groups. Each group takes a pencil and a piece of paper, and works together to write down a one sentence lead-in for a fractured fairy tale. You must include a character or scene from at least two different stories. For example, "One day Little Red Riding Hood met the Three Pigs on their way to the ball. What happened next?" Set the timer for two minutes.

2. When time is up, switch papers, and finish the stories! Set the timer for five minutes. When it goes off, share your fractured fairy tales! Vote on which was the funniest.

3. If you want, write down the stories and create illustrations to go with them. Staple them together into a book.

More Family Fun:

● International Children's Book Day falls on Hans Christian Andersen's birthday (April 2). Read some of his stories in his honor, such as *The Little Mermaid, The Steadfast Tin Soldier, The Ugly Duckling*, or *The Princess and the Pea.*

● Hold a family read-aloud-a-thon. Give all readers a chance to read aloud. See how many books you can read in an evening. Vote on your favorites.

● If you don't have a library card, sign up for one today! Spend time getting to know your library. Check out a book you have never read before.

Earth Day
(April 22)

Earth Day, first observed in 1970, is a day for all of us to think about ecology, to think of how we can better respect the earth and all its forms of life. It is observed world-wide and is also a day to think about how we can avoid pollution. Beginning back in 1955 Mister Green Jeans talked to our audience about ecology at a time when that word was new to most of us. Hugh Brannum, who was Mister Green Jeans, had a fierce devotion to the earth, its creatures, and their well-being. I never observe Earth Day without thinking of him and the message he gave to many young people before most leaders had heard messages of ecology. The environment is something we can all affect personally. The "Trash Walk" is a good example. I am certain you and your child will be able to think of many more ways you can help our environment.

Take a trash walk
(All ages)

What You'll Need:

> large grocery bags
> work gloves

> markers
> camera (optional)

Here's How to Do It:

1. Before going on your walk, decorate eye-catching trash bags so people will notice you. It may give others the idea to pick up a little trash too! Draw pictures or write slogans on the sides of large grocery bags.

2. Decide the route for your walk and how far you will go, depending on the ages of your group. A walk around the block is probably long enough for a three-year-old child.

3. Put on your work gloves, grab your bags, and head out! Keep your eyes peeled for garbage, but pay attention to the wonders of nature too. After all, that's what you're trying to save! Let grown-ups pick up broken glass and other hazardous stuff.

4. When you get back home, separate the recyclables from the trash. Before you dump the garbage in its proper place, take a snapshot of what you collected. Then wash your hands and give yourselves a high five!

More Family Fun:

- Families with school-age kids can take an Earth-care inventory of your home. Check for dripping faucets, lights left on, water heater or thermostat turned up too high, and other indicators of energy waste. Design a sorting center in part of your living space for glass, cans, plastic, and paper. If your community has a recycling program, make sure you contribute. If it doesn't, write to city officials about starting one up!

- Take a walk down an aisle in a supermarket or toy store. Look at the packaging. Sometimes there's more to the package than to the product inside! Point out examples of good packaging and bad. Talk about what you as a family can do to practice *precycling*.

- Challenge family members to reuse as much as possible. Before throwing anything away, try to think of another use for it. (Cereal boxes can be recycled into art projects. Plastic bottles can be cut down to make scoops, baskets, and toys.) Use your imagination!

Arbor Day

Arbor Day is an annual tree-planting day that was first observed on April 10, 1872, in Nebraska. The idea for such a day and the name for it were suggested by J. Sterling Morton, a member of the Nebraska Board of Agriculture and later U.S. Secretary of Agriculture. In 1885, Arbor Day was declared a legal holiday in Nebraska, where it is observed on April 22, Morton's birthday. The idea of Arbor Day spread to other states, and although the date of observance varies, it is celebrated throughout the United States. The last Friday in April has been adopted by many states as Arbor Day, and there is a movement to establish an official Arbor Day date for the whole country.

Plant a tree (All ages)

What You'll Need:

➤ a seedling
➤ a place to plant it

➤ a shovel
➤ water

Here's How to Do It:

1. Talk to the people at a nursery or gardening center to figure out what kind of tree to plant. Consider the amount of space you have and the kind of soil. How much space will the tree need when it is mature? Does it need heavy or light soil? Also ask whether it grows slowly or quickly, and how hardy the tree is for your area.

2. Because planting procedures vary from tree to tree, ask for specific planting instructions, and follow them carefully!

More Family Fun:

● If you don't have a place to plant a tree, adopt one! Find a young tree in a local park or along a boulevard that you can care for. During hot summer months, haul water to give it a drink. If you notice damaged branches or disease, alert your local parks department. If the tree is planted outside your home or apartment building, check to see if you can plant flowers around it or if you can hang a bird feeder in it. Even young children can help take care of a tree!

● Older kids can learn about the different trees in your area. You can find information at the local library or by contacting your county extension service or park service. Collect leaves from different trees and identify them. Make bark rubbings with paper and crayon. Photograph your tree in spring, summer, fall, and winter. Put it all in a scrapbook about trees.

● For more information on celebrating Arbor Day, write: National Arbor Day Foundation, Arbor Lodge 100, Nebraska City, NE 68410.

Holiday Fun

May

Activity Book

May Birthday

May is the start of the fishing season in many states. Anglers look forward to getting out on the water and reeling in the first catch. Fish also play an important part in the Boy's Day Celebration on May 5 in Japan. On that day, fish-shaped flags and kites fly from every house. For your May birthday, pick up the theme and go fishin'!

Fishy invitations and decorations

What You'll Need:

> construction paper

> crayons

> envelopes

> scissors

> waxed paper

> iron

> bobbers, fishing net or pole (optional)

> tape

> blue tablecloth or old sheet

> green tissue paper

> newspaper

Here's How to Make Them:

1. Fold construction paper into cards that will fit the envelopes. On the front of the card, draw a fish looking at a hook. Have a grown-up help you print "Don't let the big one get away!" on the front. Inside write, "Catch the fun at a Goin' Fishin' Party!" and add your party information. Mail them to your friends.

2. Decorate your party room and table with fishing gear, if you have some. Put out bobbers and nets, but no hooks! Tape construction-paper fish to a blue tablecloth and hang it in a corner of the room for a fishing game (see More Party Fun section page 105).

3. Make fishy place mats by sandwiching construction-paper fish between two layers of waxed paper. Add weeds cut from green tissue paper and add other designs with crayon. Let a grown-up seal the waxed paper together by pressing it with a warm iron. (Protect your iron and ironing board with a layer or two of newspaper.) Trim the edge of the place mat after it is sealed.

Fish cake and bait cups

What You'll Need:

- ➤ cake mix
- ➤ 9" x 13" cake pan
- ➤ vanilla cream frosting
- ➤ blue food color
- ➤ green gel icing in a tube
- ➤ green gumdrops
- ➤ yellow Lifesaver™ candy
- ➤ aluminum foil
- ➤ chocolate cookies
- ➤ board, tray, or sturdy cardboard to fit the cake
- ➤ chocolate pudding
- ➤ paper cups
- ➤ gummy worms

Here's How to Make Them:

1. With your parent's help, bake the cake, following the directions on the package for a 9" x 13" single-layer cake. Let the grown-up remove the cake from the pan to cool completely. Carefully transfer the cake to a foil-covered tray. Tint the frosting light blue with blue food coloring. Frost the top and sides of the cake. Draw a large fish shape in the middle of the cake. Cut green gumdrops to make scales and layer them on the fish. Add a yellow Lifesaver™ candy for the eye. Use gel icing to draw on weeds.

2. Fill small paper cups three-quarters full with chocolate pudding. Crumble chocolate cookies into fine "dirt" and cover the top of the pudding. Stick a couple of gummy worms in each cup. You can also serve fish-shaped snack crackers.

More Party Fun:

If you can't go fishing for real, entertain your guests with these games and activities. Choose which ones to use, depending on the ages of the kids at your party.

- Catch the worm's tail (All ages) — Play this game outside. Have everyone form a line, one behind the other. Then hold onto the waist of the person in front of you. This chain makes the worm. The object of the game is for the head of the worm to catch the tail of the worm. But the tail doesn't want to get caught! Move around your play area, wiggling and squiggling, but never letting go of the person in front of you. Take turns being the head and the tail.

- Make Japanese fish kites (All ages) — Cut a large circle out of the bottom of a paper bag. This is the fish's mouth. Scallop the other end of the bag for the tail. Draw scales and a big fish eye on the sides of the bag with a crayon. Staple colorful crepe paper streamers to the tail. Punch two holes in the bottom of the sack, in the corners above the mouth. Tie string through the holes. You can attach the string to a dowel, or you can hold onto it and run with your kite.

● Fish pole game (Ages 3-5 and 6-7) — Hang a sheet in a corner of the room. Make a fish pole from a dowel and yarn. Tie a paper clip to the end for a hook. Let kids take turns "casting" the line over the sheet. Have someone on the other side attach a small prize to the paper clip and then tug on the line. This signals the fisherman to pull it in and see what he or she caught!

● Catch a big one (Ages 3-5 and 6-7) — Cut several fish shapes from foam food trays. Write a number from one to five on one side of each fish. Tape a plastic curtain ring to the other side. Float the fish in a tub of water or a wading pool. (See the game above for making fish poles.) Let players take turns catching three fish. Add up the numbers on the backs of the three fish caught. The person with the highest score wins.

● Swim in schools (Ages 6-7 and 8-10) — Play this game in a large area. Begin by having everyone just run around. Then shout a number between two and 10 (or the number of guests). Players must stop running and quickly form groups of that number by holding onto one another. As soon as groups form, shout "Go!" and everybody runs around again. Then call a different number. (It's okay if the numbers don't work out just right. The fun of the game is the scramble to connect!)

● Go looking for the real thing! (All ages) — If it's possible, go fishing for real, or visit an aquarium or fish store. Then come back to your house for refreshments.

May Day
(May 1)

May Day is based on the Roman holiday, Floralia, and is celebrated in most European countries. As with the Roman holiday, May Day celebrates the coming of springtime in the Northern Hemisphere. The holiday involves baskets of flowers and dancing around a "maypole." The More Family Fun section contains directions for making a maypole.

Make a May basket from a plastic bottle

(Ages 3-5 and 6-7)

What You'll Need:

- ➤ plastic 2-liter soda bottle
- ➤ chenille stick (pipe cleaner)
- ➤ thin ribbon or yarn
- ➤ scissors
- ➤ paper punch
- ➤ masking tape
- ➤ small potted flowering plant or fresh or silk flowers

Here's How to Make It:

1. Let a grown-up cut off the bottom third of the bottle and dispose of the top. Punch holes about an inch apart along the top edge of the basket.

2. Decorate the basket by weaving thin ribbon or yarn through the holes. (Wrap a small piece of masking tape around the end of the ribbon or yarn to keep it from fraying.) Tie a pretty bow in the front.

3. Twist a chenille stick (pipe cleaner) on for a handle. Fill the pot with flowers or pop in a small potted plant.

4. Surprise a neighbor or friend with the basket. Leave it by the door and ring the bell or knock. Quickly run and hide! (But you might want to peek to see the happy smile on the person's face!)

More Family Fun:

● May Day is celebrated in many different ways throughout the world. In Italy they hold sports meets, races, and contests. Plan a sports day in your neighborhood. Run fun races: three-legged relays, wheelbarrow races, and sack races. Enjoy the warmer days and more hours of sunshine!

● Erect a maypole in your yard! Attach crepe paper streamers to the top of a clothesline pole, making sure there's a streamer for each person. Have each person grab the end of a streamer. Play a recording of happy music and dance around the pole!

Lei Day
(May 1)

In Hawaii, May 1 is Lei Day, not May Day. Make a lei to celebrate!

Make a lei (Ages 3-5 and 6-7)

What You'll Need:

➤ yarn

➤ construction paper

➤ foam food trays

➤ straws

➤ plastic darning needle

➤ button

➤ scissors

Here's How to Make It:

1. Cut 24" or 36" lengths of yarn. Tie one end of the yarn onto a plastic darning needle to keep it from slipping off. Tie a button to the other end of the yarn.

2. Cut straws into one-inch lengths. Cut flower shapes from construction paper and foam food trays. Let a grown-up help you punch holes in the center of each flower with the plastic needle.

3. String the flower shapes onto the yarn, alternating between paper and foam, putting a straw spacer between each. When you are within two inches of the end, remove the needle and tie the yarn ends together. Place the lei around your neck (or give it to someone else). Aloha!

More Family Fun:

● Try this with older kids: Did you know that there are only twelve letters in the Hawaiian alphabet? (A, E, I, O, U, H, K, L, M, N, P, and W). How many words can you spell using only those letters? Try writing a story with the words!

● Grow a pineapple plant. Have your parent help you cut off the top of a fresh pineapple about an inch below the leaves. Scoop the fruit out of the part you cut off. (Save the bottom for a snack.) Place the top on a plate and let it dry for a few days. Then plant it in a pot of damp, sandy soil. Don't bury it too deep in the soil— leave the top part uncovered. Keep the soil damp. Pretty soon roots will start to grow. You might even get a new pineapple to form eventually!

● For more Hawaiian ideas, turn to pages 134-38.

Cinco De Mayo
(May 5)

Cinco de Mayo is a national holiday in Mexico, but Mexicans everywhere celebrate it. The holiday commemorates the anniversary of the Battle of Puebla on May 5, 1962, when Mexican troops, outnumbered three to one, defeated Napoleon's French army. On Cinco de Mayo, there are parades and music and dancing. Celebrate Cinco de Mayo with your own family fiesta!

Papier mâché maraca

(Ages 8-10)

What You'll Need:

- flour
- salt
- large bowl
- burned out light bulb
- paint brush
- lukewarm water
- spoon
- old newspapers
- acrylic paint
- clear finish spray

Here's How to Make It:

1. Mix the flour and water a little at a time in a large bowl. The mixture should be a soupy paste. When you get it just right, add a dash of salt to the mixture.

2. Tear newspapers into one-inch strips. Dip the strips in the paste to coat them. Use your fingers to squeeze off any extra globs of paste. Wrap the strips around the light bulb in a crisscross pattern, so that they overlap. Cover the entire surface of the bulb. Add a second layer.

3. Let the bulb dry for several hours. Repeat the process *at least* two more times, for a total of *six* layers. The coating must be thick and strong. If you are in doubt, add another layer!

4. After the final layer is dry, have an adult hit the bulb on a hard surface. This will break the light bulb inside, but should not harm the papier mâché coating. The broken pieces inside will make the rattling sound for your maraca!

5. Paint colorful designs on the maraca and let it dry. Then spray it with a clear finish to protect it.

More Family Fun:

● Go through your cookbooks and plan a Mexican meal to celebrate Cinco De Mayo! Decorate your table with colorful streamers. See pages 179-83 for more fiesta ideas!

International Tuba Day

(First Friday in May)

Calling all musicians! Grab your instrument and join the band! Don't have a tuba? Make a kazoo!

Paper tube kazoo

(Ages 3-5 and 6-7)

What You'll Need:

➤ paper towel tube

➤ rubber band

➤ markers

➤ waxed paper

➤ scissors

Here's How to Make It:

1. Cut the tube down to about five inches.

2. Draw designs or finger holes on the tube.

3. Cover the end of the tube with waxed paper and secure it tightly with a rubber band.

4. Punch a small hole in the top of the tube.

5. Put the open end of the tube over your mouth and hum with your mouth open.

More Family Fun:

● John Philip Sousa wrote music especially suited for the tuba. Check out some Sousa recordings from the library. Gather whatever pretend or real instruments you may have in your house and play along.

National Teacher Day

(First Tuesday of the first full week in May)

Teachers are very influential people in the lives of children, but are often underappreciated. National Teacher Day provides an opportunity for children and parents to express their thanks to teachers. From the early-childhood teacher to the elementary and secondary school teachers, the influence these people have on our children is enormous. When I was young, "an apple for the teacher," was a common expression; it reminded us to say "thank you." The activities below will help you express your gratitude, and, of course, a simple "thank you" expressed in person can lift any teacher's spirits. Teachers share with parents the responsibility for nurturing and educating children. It is an awesome responsibility. The best thanks a teacher can receive is the understanding and support of parents. And it is the children who truly benefit from such a parental attitude.

Design an apple print thank-you card for your favorite teacher!

(Ages 6-7 and 8-10)

What You'll Need:

- ➤ an apple
- ➤ white construction paper
- ➤ paper plate or pie pan
- ➤ markers
- ➤ sharp knife
- ➤ red paint
- ➤ newspaper

Here's How to Make It:

1. Let a grown-up slice the apple in half from top to bottom. Wipe off the surface of the apple.

2. Cover your work area with newspaper. Pour a small amount of red paint on the paper plate or in the bottom of your pie pan. You only need enough paint to cover the cut edge of the apple.

3. Fold the construction paper in half to make a card. Dip the cut side of the apple in the paint. Blot off excess paint by pressing lightly on the newspaper. Then press the apple firmly on the front of your card.

4. Let the paint dry, then add a stem and leaves with a marker. You might also want to write something on the front of the card, such as "Thank You!" or "To My Favorite Teacher!"

5. Open the card and write a note, telling your teacher why you enjoyed being in his or her class this year. Your teacher will appreciate it!

More Family Fun:

● Would you like to give more than a card? You can put apple prints on many things. If you use fabric paints, you can print on T-shirts, canvas bags, caps, or just about anything made from cloth. You might even want to frame an apple print to hang on a wall. Have your parent help you create a whole orchard of apple prints.

International Day of Families
(May 15)

What could be more important than your family? As adults, everything we do, is designed to strengthen the family and make each member secure and happy in the family environment. Children need a sense of belong-ing, they need to understand relationships within the extended family. The "family book" suggested here allows a child to become more familiar with members of his or her extended family. The "family tree" provides a graphic means of showing relationships. As important as ethnic pride may be, pride in family is very important as well. The basic unit of society is the family and children need to know more about their family and just where their place in the family happens to be. While engaging in these activities, talk about your family. Talk about how Aunt Sue is your sister and share some of the fun you had with her growing up. It is difficult for a child to think of a parent as having been a small child but that understanding gives a child confidence that he or she, too, will grow and become an adult. Talk about family on other days of the year. Pride in family is an important element in building security and self-esteem in a child.

Take pride in your family! Create a "This Is Our Family" book together
(Ages 6-7 and 8-10)

What You'll Need:

- ➤ loose-leaf binder
- ➤ paper punch
- ➤ scissors
- ➤ family photographs
- ➤ construction paper
- ➤ transparent tape
- ➤ glue
- ➤ markers or crayons

Here's How to Make It:

1. First, make some pages for your family scrapbook. Run transparent tape along one side of each piece of construction paper to reinforce it. Then punch holes in the paper so it will fit into the binder.

2. Give each family member a page and have them draw a self-portrait. On the back of the portrait, write down information about the person, such as his or her birthday, nickname, favorite food, hobby—whatever! Glue a photograph of the person onto the page.

3. Create other pages for your book. You might want to assign pages to different family members. You could paste in photos of family vacations and outings; list your family's rules; include a secret recipe; or draw a map of your house or apartment. Use your imagination—what makes your family special?

4. Draw a family tree and plot what you know about your family's history. Where did your ancestors come from? What did they do for a living? Do you have photos of family members no longer living? Paste them in the book! Give everyone a chance to contribute something.

5. When you have completed all the pages, assemble them in the binder. Then sit down and read the book together. You might learn something new about yourselves!

More Family Fun:

- Plan a family outing for International Family Day. Visit a museum or history center, or a favorite park. Do whatever your family enjoys! Remember to take a camera along to record the day. When you get the pictures developed, you can add them to a page in your family book.

- Take turns honoring individual family members once a week with a special meal. Let the person honored choose the menu, sit at the head of the table, and get out of doing dishes for one day!

Mother's Day
(Second Sunday in May)

Many of you remember how the Captain ended many programs with reminder to the children that "this is another be good to mother day." The point, of course, was that every day is another "be good to mother day." In 1914, by presidential proclamation, this day was  set aside to honor mothers and show appreciation for all they do in nurturing children throughout the year. It is an exciting day for children because every child has a natural, strong and binding love for mother. Young children look with delight to this special day on which they are able, through special acts and activities, to show a special love. Perhaps this book, opened to this page, should be made available to the male parent so that he can be guided in helping the child celebrate this important day in the life of any child. Next month we'll open the book to Father's Day and Mother can help guide that celebration.

Honor Mom with a special place mat! (All ages)

What You'll Need:

- 12" x 18" construction paper or paper place mat
- clear-adhesive backed vinyl
- old greeting cards
- glue
- paper scraps
- photograph of you and Mom
- scissors
- markers or crayons

Here's How to Make It:

1. Glue the photograph of you and your mom in the center of a 12" x 18" piece of construction paper or paper place mat.

2. Cut pretty pictures from greeting cards or free-hand designs from paper and arrange them collage-style around the photo. When you're happy with the arrangement, glue the pictures to the mat.

3. Add any message you want or color on any additional designs. You might even compose a poem for Mom!

4. Before using the mat, cover both sides with clear adhesive-backed vinyl. This will keep it protected for years to come!

More Family Fun:

● Do the cooking for Mom today. Prepare her favorite meal and serve it up on the place mat you made. Remember to do the dishes for her too!

● Moms wearing carnations is a Mother's Day tradition. Make a bouquet of tissue paper carnations to give your mother. Cut red tissue paper with a pinking shears into 4" squares. Layer 5 squares and fold them together accordian style. Wrap a green chenille stick (pipe cleaner) tightly around the middle for a stem. Carefully pull up each layer of tissue toward the center to form the flower.

● On Mother's Day (and everyday) try speaking these words Mom likes to hear. Her smile will will brighten your day!
1. Please?
2. Thank you.
3. May I clear the table?
4. I'm going to do my homework (or clean my room) now.
5. I love you, Mom!

● A special day honoring mothers is celebrated in many countries, including Denmark, Finland, Italy, Turkey, Australia, Belgium, Sweden, and England. In Mexico, it lasts two days. Why not make Mother's Day last a week this year? Or better yet, let Mom know you love her every day!

● Mother's Day falls just in time for garden planting. For a fun activity, go with your mother to a gardening center and buy some bedding plants and potting soil. Then work with her to create a pretty container garden for your patio, steps, or porch. Work together to take care of the garden throughout the summer. Just like flowers will flourish with tender loving care, so do our relationships!

● Before you go to bed tonight, crawl into Mom's lap and share a story and a hug! You might want to make up a story to tell your mom and ask her to tell you one.

Memorial Day
(Last Monday in May)

Very young children have difficulty understanding the concept of death, the sacrifice of people before us who made such a contribution to our nation and its security. What children can understand is pride. Use this day to instill a sense of pride in this nation and its principles. A discussion of how fortunate we are to live in a society that allows us to speak out and to worship as we wish is appropriate today. Also appropriate today is a discussion of our responsibilities. Parents often tell children about their rights but fail to talk about the accompanying responsibilities that are part of the exercise of those rights. We have the right to free speech, but it must be responsible speech. Speech that promotes hate and ill-feelings toward others is not responsible. We have the right to certain activities in play and in school but we also have a responsibility to consider the rights of others in those activities. The sacrifices made by the people we honor today are meaningful only if we live the sort of life that they made possible. A parent or adult who teaches responsibility as well as rights is doing so in a fine American tradition.

Create a poppy tribute
(Ages 8-10)

What You'll Need:

➤ plastic-foam wreath (available at craft stores)

➤ red, white, and blue fabric scraps

➤ red ribbon

➤ light-weight wire

➤ red and green crepe paper streamers

➤ black chenille stems (pipe cleaners)

➤ pencil

➤ scissors

Here's How to Make It:

1. Cut the fabric into two-inch squares.

2. Place a fabric square on the wreath. Poke the center of it into the foam with the point of a pencil. Continue until the front and sides are covered with fabric. Alternate the colors so you have a random pattern.

3. To make a paper poppy, fold a chenille stem in half. Cut two two-inch circles from red crepe paper. Poke a hole in the middle of each and pull them onto the chenille stem until they almost reach the folded end. Pinch the base of the red petals slightly, and starting at the base, wrap green crepe paper around the chenille stem until it is covered completely.

4. Make several poppies and tie them together with a red ribbon. Attach your poppy bouquet to the wreath with wire.

5. Hang the wreath on your door as a tribute to the men and women who have served our country.

More Family Fun:

Families with school-age kids might want to observe Memorial Day in one of these ways:

● Veteran's groups throughout the United States make and sell poppies each year around Memorial Day. Instead of making poppies for your wreath, you might wish to buy some from one of the veteran's organizations.

● Find a copy of the poem "In Flander's Fields" and read it together. The poem remembers soldiers who fought and died during World War I.

● Spend some time on Memorial Day remembering relatives and friends who are no longer living. You might look through family photo albums or visit the graves of loved ones.

● Attend a local Memorial Day observance. Veteran's organizations often hold services of some kind on this day. If you live near a national cemetery, there is most likely a service featuring a color guard, band, and speakers.

● Is there a parade on this day in your town or in a nearby community? Grab or make an American flag and stand watching the parade. (See page 139, Flag Day.)

June

Activity Book

June
Birthday

Hold a party with a tropical flair! Take your guests on an imaginary trip to Hawaii to celebrate your birthday this year!

Shell invitations and party decorations

What You'll Need:

- construction paper
- tissue paper
- green crepe paper streamers
- wide green ribbon
- basket or large bowl
- assorted real or plastic tropical fruit
- scissors
- stapler
- markers

Here's How to Make Them:

1. Invitations: Cut 9" x 12" pieces of light-colored construction paper in half. Fold each piece in half to make a card. Cut a scallop shell shape from each card, placing the hinge of the shell along the fold. Open the card and write your invitation inside. (If you are planning to hold your party outside, you may want to invite your guests to bring along their swimming suits.)

2. Decorations: Make place mats by gluing tissue paper flower shapes collage-style onto white construction paper. Make hula skirts for everyone by stapling green crepe paper streamers to wide ribbon to tie around their waists. At the party, let your guests make leis to wear and take home as favors. (See the instructions on page 111.) In addition, many party goods stores also carry items with a tropical theme, if you wish to buy some other party favors or decorations.

Lei cake, tropical fruit kabobs, and party punch

What You'll Need:

➤ 9" x 13" cake pan

➤ cake mix

➤ board, tray, or heavy cardboard, big enough to fit the cake

➤ aluminum foil

➤ vanilla cream or fluffy white frosting

➤ yellow food coloring

➤ large marshmallows

➤ gum drops

➤ birthday candles

➤ kitchen shears

➤ assorted fresh fruits (pineapple, banana, strawberries, melon)

➤ bamboo skewers

➤ pineapple juice

➤ cranberry juice

➤ ginger ale

➤ crushed ice

Here's How to Make Them:

1. Help your parent to bake the cake, following the directions on the package for a 9" x 13" single layer. Let your parent remove the cake from the pan to cool completely. Carefully transfer it to a foil-covered tray or board. Add food coloring to the frosting to make it bright yellow. Frost the top and sides of the cake. Then cut large marshmallows into four pieces each with a kitchen shear. (The cut pieces will look like flower petals.) Position five petals around gumdrop centers to make flowers. (If you want different colors of flowers, dip the sticky sides of the marshmallow petals in colored sugar.) Arrange the flowers on the top of the cake in the shape of a lei. Stick birthday candles in the centers of a few of the flowers, in place of gumdrops.

2. Fruit kabobs: Wash the strawberries and cut fresh pineapple, melons, and bananas into chunks. (Canned pineapple chunks may be substituted, if well drained.) Push a piece of each kind of fruit onto a bamboo skewer. Make a kabob for each guest. Turn a melon half upside down on a platter and stick the pointed ends of the skewers into the rind for a table centerpiece.

3. Party punch: Combine a quart of cranberry juice with two quarts of pineapple juice. Add a quart of ginger ale and pour into glasses of crushed ice. Stick in a straw and a paper umbrella, if you have some!

More Party Fun:

Entertain your party guests with these games and activities. Choose which ones to use, depending on the ages of your guests.

● Do the limbo! (All ages) — Grab a broom or a long pole, put on some music, and get ready to dance! Have two people hold the broom while everyone else dances under it. Each time around, lower the broom a little. See how low you can go without falling on your back!

● Bowling pineapples (Ages 3-5) — Make five "pineapples" by taping green paper leaves to the tops of 2-liter plastic soda bottles covered with brown paper. Arrange them in a triangle and take turns rolling a small ball at them. Let everyone have several turns. Keep score by counting how many bottles fall down.

● Tropical fish toss (Ages 3-5 and 6-7) — Cut out five or six large fish shapes from construction paper. Number the fish from 1 to 5, writing the numeral on with a dark marker. (If you have a fish for each guest, you could let your guests color the fish before you play.) Tape the fish to the floor, leaving a few inches of space between them. Stand six feet away (or closer for young children) and take turns tossing a bean bag toward the fish. Each person gets three tosses. Add up the numbers—the person with the highest score wins.

● Sugar cube tumble (Ages 6-7 and 8-10) — Build a tower of sugar cubes made from one of Hawaii's biggest crops—sugar cane! Give each player a pile of sugar cubes. Build a tower together, taking turns adding a cube. Stack the cubes as high as you can. But watch out—if your cube makes the tower fall, you're out!

● Outdoor fun (All ages) — Fill your wading pool or turn on your backyard sprinkler and cool off! If you want, hold part of your party at your local swimming pool and return to your house for refreshments—what could be easier?

Flag Day

(June 14)

Flag Day is day filled with myths about our nation's flag and a day when parents can emphasize the meaning of that flag around the world. Perhaps you can talk to your child about how Flag Day was celebrated when you were young and the things you did in school. When I was in elementary school there were only 48 stars on the flag. Why was that? What do the thirteen stripes on the flag mean? The flag is older than our constitution; it was adopted in 1777 by the Second Continental Congress meeting in Philadelphia. When we pledge allegiance to the flag are we pledging ourselves to a piece of cloth or, as the pledge states, "to the republic for which it stands, one nation, under God . . ." We pledge to uphold that nation that cannot be divided and that guarantees liberty and justice for all. Pledging allegiance is easy; living that pledge is what is important.

Design your own flag

(Ages 6-7 and 8-10)

What You'll Need:

➤ construction paper
➤ scissors
➤ dowel

➤ crayons or markers
➤ glue

Here's How to Make It:

1. Decide first what shape you want your flag. It doesn't have to be a rectangle. You might want to make it a triangle or square shape. What colors will you include? What symbols or designs? You might want to look up flags of the world in an encyclopedia to give you some ideas.

2. Cut your paper into its desired shape. Then color on designs or cut them from paper and glue them on.

3. Once you are happy with your flag, glue it to a dowel so you can wave it proudly!

More Family Fun:

● If you own a U.S. flag, fly it on Flag Day! You can buy flag kits for a reasonable price at most discount stores this time of year. Even if you live in an apartment, you can display a small American flag in a window.

● Take a trip around your neighborhood or community and count the number of flags.

● Learn the Pledge of Allegiance and recite it together or sing "The Star Spangled Banner," "America the Beautiful," or "You're a Grand Old Flag."

● Read a book about Betsy Ross or look up information about her in an encyclopedia. Find out the significance of the stars and stripes and the colors of the flag.

● Find out the proper ways to display and take care of the flag.

San Juan Bautista Day

(June 24)

T his saint's day has a special place in the hearts of Puerto Ricans. Christopher Columbus named their island San Jaun Bautista in 1493. The capital city still bears the name San Juan. The night before the feast day, families gather on the beach for food and singing and dancing. When midnight comes, they take their first dip in the ocean for the summer—by walking backwards into the sea! The custom is supposed to bring you blessings from St. John (San Juan), so that you will have a safe and happy year.

Plan a backyard beach party (Ages 3-5)

What You'll Need:

➤ wading pool

➤ beach towels

➤ cassette player and tapes of lively music

➤ favorite snacks

➤ crepe paper streamers

Here's How to Do It:

1. Decorate your yard with colorful streamers. Cut streamers for everybody to wave. Prepare easy snacks like bananas and orange slices and lemonade. Fill your wading pool with water, and set it by a sandbox, if you have one. Put out water and sand toys to play with.

2. Then invite your friends over, and remind them to bring their swimsuits and towels.

3. Have a spontaneous celebration! Put on music for dancing. Give everyone a streamer to wave. At the planned time, have everyone jump in the pool! (You don't have to wait until midnight!)

More Family Fun:

● If you do live near a beach, plan a get-together with another family or two. Arrange for music and games and have everyone bring food to share.

● Spanish is the language spoken in Puerto Rico. Learn some friendly Spanish greetings: "¡Hola!" (Hello!), "¡Buenos dias!" (Good day!), "¡Buenos tardes!" (Good afternoon!), "¡Buenos nocas!" (Good evening!) "¿Cómo estás?" (How are you?)

● Guitar music is a popular part of San Juan Bautista celebrations in Puerto Rico. Does anyone you know play guitar? Invite that person over to sing some songs with you!

Father's Day
(Third Sunday in June)

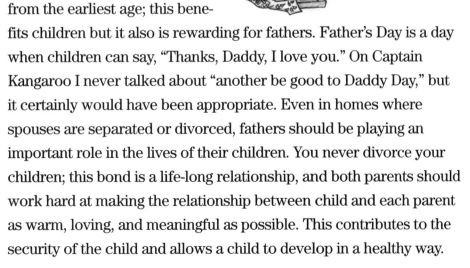

Fathers have a critical role to play in the nurturing of children. In these days of both parents working outside the home, the Father's role has assumed an even greater importance. Fathers can be seen nurturing children from the earliest age; this bene-fits children but it also is rewarding for fathers. Father's Day is a day when children can say, "Thanks, Daddy, I love you." On Captain Kangaroo I never talked about "another be good to Daddy Day," but it certainly would have been appropriate. Even in homes where spouses are separated or divorced, fathers should be playing an important role in the lives of their children. You never divorce your children; this bond is a life-long relationship, and both parents should work hard at making the relationship between child and each parent as warm, loving, and meaningful as possible. This contributes to the security of the child and allows a child to develop in a healthy way.

Father's Day affords the opportunity to strengthen the natural bond between father and child. This is good for Dad, good for Mom and very good for the child.

A hand-made tie (All ages)

He might not wear it, but this gift is sure to make him smile!

What You'll Need:

- ➤ an old tie (pick one up at a garage sale!)
- ➤ felt pieces in different colors
- ➤ pen
- ➤ fabric paint (optional)
- ➤ scissors
- ➤ fabric or craft glue

Here's How to Make It:

1. Have someone help you trace your hands onto different colors of felt and cut them out. You will need three or four shapes, depending on the size of your hand.

2. Position the hands on the wide end of the tie. Overlap them slightly. Glue the hand shapes to the tie.

3. Use fabric paints to add fingernails or other decorations, if you wish. If more than one person has contributed a hand print, write your names on the hands.

4. Present Dad with your "handsome" gift!

More Family Fun:

- Make a "Handy Helper" coupon book for Father's Day. Cut hand prints from several pieces of construction paper and staple them together into a booklet. On each coupon print something for which Dad may receive in exchange, such as "Good for one hug" or "Good for an hour of yard work."

- Spend time with your dad today. Take a walk together, read a story, or play a game. Let Dad choose what to do.

- Ask your dad to share stories of when he was young. What are some of his most favorite memories? Look through old photo albums together, and talk about what it was like being a kid then.

- Start a hobby with your dad. Maybe choose something neither of you has tried before. You could collect stamps, hunt for rocks or shells, go birdwatching, or build stuff in the workshop.

- Teach Dad a new game you have just learned. Or ask him to teach you one!

- Host a "Father/Child Olympics" on Father's Day this year. Invite the dads and kids in your neighborhood to participate. Run three-legged, sack, and wheelbarrow races, do a water balloon toss, and play other crazy games. Give medals to all the fathers for being "super dads." (See pages 257-58, Noble Prize Awards, for instructions on making medals.)

Holiday Fun

July

Activity Book

July Birthday

Rock and roll at your very own malt shop! Celebrate your birthday '50s style!

Record invitation and malt shop party decorations

What You'll Need:

- black construction paper
- plain white paper
- empty plastic 35 mm film canister
- business-size envelopes
- large cardboard box
- aluminum foil
- shelf paper
- posterboard
- markers
- glue
- pencil
- scissors

Here's How to Make Them:

1. Invitations: For each invitation, cut a seven-inch diameter circle from black construction paper. Cut two five-inch circles from white paper. Glue the white circles to the middle of the black circle (one on each side). Place a 35 mm film canister (or object similar in size) in the center of the white circle and trace around it. Cut out the little circle. You've cut a record! Title your hit song, "Happy Birthday to (Name)" and add your party information to the record label. Invite your guests to wear their favorite '50s fashions and meet you at the malt shop! (Note: You will have to fold your records to fit them into business-size envelopes.) If you want, make some more records to hang around your party area.

2. Jukebox: Cover a large cardboard box with shelf paper and glue on shiny music notes and records cut from aluminum foil and construction paper. Draw on buttons and a record menu. Cut a slot in the box to insert coins. You can give your guests pretend coins cut from posterboard and covered with foil to use to "play" the jukebox. (Have a cassette player nearby with a cassette of '50s music to turn on or tune your radio to a golden oldies' station!)

3. Cover your table with a red-checked plastic tablecloth or set up your kitchen counter as a soda fountain. Let your guests order treats from a menu that lists your party food. You could serve hot dogs and chips or burgers and fries. And don't forget to include milkshakes!

Autograph cake

In the '50s, autograph books were the rage. Bake an autograph cake, and let your guests help decorate it!

What You'll Need:

➤ 9" x 13" cake pan
➤ cake mix
➤ vanilla cream frosting
➤ tray, board, or sturdy cardboard, large enough to fit the cake

➤ aluminum foil
➤ assorted colors of gel icing in tubes
➤ birthday candles

Here's How to Make It:

1. With a grown-up's help, bake the cake, following the directions on the package for a single 9" x 13" layer. Let the adult remove the cake from the pan to cool completely. Then carefully transfer it to a foil-covered tray or board. Frost the top and sides, making the frosting as smooth as you can.

2. At the party, have tubes of icing available, and let guests sign their names or initials on the cake. (Have a grown-up or an older kid write on the names for younger children.) Just before serving, stick in your birthday candles.

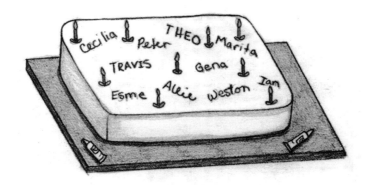

More Party Fun:

Get your party rockin' with these games and activities. Choose which ones to use, depending on the ages of your guests.

- Hula Hoop Game (All ages) — One hula hoop is needed for this game. Players form a line, holding hands. The first person in line steps into the hula hoop and then attempts to move the hoop to the next person without dropping hands! Try to get the hoop from one end of the line to the other without anyone dropping hands. It can be done!

- Cruisin' (Ages 3-5) — You will need a toy car for this activity. (A T-bird convertible is perfect, but any car will do!) Sit in a circle, and scoot the car back and forth between players. You can use the game to help guests learn each other's names, by calling out a person's name before you send the car rolling. Or you can go through the alphabet or count each time the car cruises across. Make sure everyone gets a chance to "drive" the car.

- Autograph Books (Ages 6-7 and 8-10) — Before the party, assemble an autograph book for each guest. Cut a piece of construction paper in half to make a front and a back cover. Sandwich several pages of plain paper in between (have at least as many pages as you have guests). Staple along one short end of the book. Write "Autographs" on the front cover. At the party, spend time writing in each other's books. Make up verses like, "Roses and red, violets are blue. There's no better friend in the world than you!" or "2-Nice 2-B 4-Gotten!" Ask a grown-up what verses he or she remembers. At the end of the party, the guests can take their books home.

- Sock Hop (Ages 6-7) — Set up two chairs on one side of the room. Line up in two teams on the other side. (If you don't have an equal number of people, have a person on the short team go twice.) Give a large tube sock to the first person in each line. At the starting signal, have them slip the sock over one shoe and hop on the other foot across the room, around the chair, and back again. Then pass the sock to the next person in line and repeat. The first team to finish, wins.

- Bubble Gum Race (Ages 8-10) — Give each player a piece of bubble gum that has been in the refrigerator for some time. (Make sure it's cold!) See who can be the first to thaw the gum, chew it up, and blow a bubble!

- Fifties' Fun (All ages) — Invite kids to bring their roller skates or inline skates and go skating during your party. You could go to a roller rink or just skate around on the sidewalks. Another easy idea is to gather a bunch of hula hoops and hold a contest. Don't forget the music—put on '50s classics and dance the party away!

Independence Day

(July 4)

By June of 1776 the American colonies were pretty upset by the grievous treatment they had been receiving at the hands of King George III and a congress of the colonies, The Continental Congress, was convened in Philadelphia. There was consensus that the colonies needed to declare themselves free of the British Crown, an independent nation. A committee, headed by Thomas

Jefferson, was appointed and on July 4th, 1776, the Continental Congress adopted this Declaration of Independence. This, then, is the date that marks the birthday of our nation. Children may not have the knowledge and experience to be politically sophisticated but they do understand what a birthday means. Use this joyous day to allow children to celebrate the birthday of their country. Happy Birthday to us all!

Hold a neighborhood parade! (All ages)

What You'll Need:

➤ streamers

➤ masking tape

➤ balloons

➤ wagon, bike, or trike

➤ assorted musical instruments or materials to make them

➤ dowels or sticks

Here's How to Do It:

1. Organize your friends and family. Set a time for the parade and let everyone know. Make it part of a Fourth of July block party! Plan a route for the parade. Check with a grown-up to see if you can block off the street for a while or use a vacant church or school parking lot. If you can't, be safe and stick to the sidewalk.

2. Decorate your bike or trike by weaving streamers through the wheel spokes and taping them to the handle bars. Turn your wagon into a float by taping streamers and balloons all around. Stick your favorite stuffed toys or dolls in the wagon and make miniature flags for them to wave (see page 139, Flag Day). Or put a ribbon on your pet and pull him or her in the parade. Be creative!

3. If you don't have wheels, assemble a marching band! Gather real or toy instruments or make some from stuff you have around the house. Coffee cans make great drums and pan lids are perfect cymbals. (See pages 114 and 116 for directions on making other instruments.)

4. Dress up in costumes, if you want, and attach flags or balloons and streamers to dowels. Pass them out to spectators along the way.

5. When everything is ready, assemble at the beginning of the route and let the parade begin!

More Family Fun:

● Attend a community fireworks display. Take lawn chairs or a blanket along and don't forget the insect repellent!

● Have a "Happy Birthday America" party. Make cupcakes and sprinkle them with red, white, and blue candy confetti. With parents helping, light a candle in each. Invite everyone to make a personal wish for the country. Then blow out the candles together.

National Ice Cream Day
(Third Sunday in July)

July can be the hottest month of the year. What better time to celebrate a day devoted to a cold delight—ice cream! If you like cones or sundaes of banana splits, this is a holiday for you. Grab your bowls and spoons and celebrate National Ice Cream Day!

Make your own ice cream!
(Ages 6-7 and 8-10)

What You'll Need:

➤ 2 cups sugar

➤ juice from 2 lemons

➤ 1 pint heavy cream

➤ 1 quart whole milk

➤ 2 cups chopped fruit

➤ large mixing bowl

➤ ice

➤ spoon

➤ rock salt

➤ electric or crank-type ice cream maker

➤ bowls and spoons

Here's How to Do It:

1. Mix together in a large bowl, the sugar, lemon juice, and cream. Add two cups of your favorite chopped fruit. (Strawberries, raspberries, or peaches are good choices!)

2. Pour the mixture into your ice cream freezer container and add milk to fill the container. Insert the dasher and put on the lid. Put the container in the ice cream freezer.

3. Pour crushed ice around the tank and sprinkle rock salt over it. Turn on the freezer or start cranking! You'll have a frosty dessert in no time!

Cone critters (All ages)

You don't have an ice cream freezer? You can still celebrate National Ice Cream Day with a delicious ice cream treat. Try making Cone Critters!

What You'll Need:

- ice cream
- scoop
- ice cream cones
- vanilla wafers
- gum drops, chocolate chips, or jelly beans
- licorice whips

Here's How to Make Them:

1. Pack a large scoop of ice into a cone. Make sure it will not fall out.

2. Create a critter by adding candy or chocolate chips for eyes and nose. You can cut licorice whips into whiskers or mouths.

3. Stick a couple of vanilla wafers in for ears, and you're ready to eat! Yum!

More Family Fun:

● Invite your neighbors over for an ice cream social. Set out several kinds of ice cream and lots of tasty toppings. See who can make the most unusual ice cream sundae!

● Play "Tutti-fruity"—an ice cream version of "Fruit Basket Upset." You need at least seven players, but it's more fun with a big group. Count off by threes. All ones are chocolate; all twos, vanilla; and all threes, strawberry. Find a chair for each person, minus one. Arrange them in a large circle. Choose one person to stand in the middle and be the caller. The rest sit down. The caller begins by shouting out one of the flavors of ice cream. Players who belong to the flavor named quickly switch chairs with someone else, while the caller tries to gain a seat for himself or herself. The person left without a chair is the next caller. Flavors can be called in any order. Watch out—if the caller shouts "Tutti-Fruity!" *everyone* must find a new chair!

August

Activity Book

August Birthday

E ach year, the first week in August is celebrated as International Clown Week. For your August birthday, hold a party under the big top!

Balloon invitations and clown table favors

What You'll Need:

- balloons
- envelopes
- permanent marker
- small slips of paper
- cardboard tubes

- craft sticks
- construction paper and tissue paper scraps
- cone-shaped party hats
- pompoms

Here's How to Make Them:

1. Invitations: Blow up a balloon, but don't tie it. Hold the end (or ask someone to help you) so air won't escape while you write your party invitation on the balloon with a permanent marker. Deflate the balloon and stick it in an envelope. Write a note on a slip of paper telling the recipient to blow up the balloon for a message. Stick the note in the envelope too. Make a balloon invitation for each guest, and mail them.

2. Clown table favors: Let your guests make party puppets from toilet paper tubes, craft sticks and paper scraps. Glue or tape the craft stick inside the tube for a handle. Cover the tube with construction paper. Then cut out eyes, nose, and mouth from paper scraps and glue them on. Make funny hair by shredding and crumpling up tissue paper and taping it to the top of the tube. Add a crepe paper ruffle around the bottom and you're all set for a party puppet show!

3. Glue big pompoms to cone-shaped party hats for the clowns at your party to wear. Glue on other decorations as you wish.

Circus tent cake and ice cream clowns

What You'll Need:

- ➤ cake mix
- ➤ vanilla cream or fluffy frosting
- ➤ round cake pans
- ➤ large plate
- ➤ orange slices
- ➤ birthday candles
- ➤ small candies

- ➤ yellow and red food coloring
- ➤ frosted animal cookies
- ➤ red licorice twists
- ➤ sugar cones
- ➤ vanilla ice cream
- ➤ paper cup cake liners

Here's How to Make Them:

1. Follow the directions on the cake mix for baking a two-layer, round cake. With a parent helping, remove the layers from the pans and let them cool completely. Carefully transfer one layer to a plate and spread vanilla frosting over the top. Put on the second layer. Tint a cup of vanilla frosting with yellow and red food coloring to make a bright orange. Spread that over the top of the cake. Frost the sides of the cake with white frosting. Make a scalloped edge at the top of the cake with orange slices. Press animal cookies all around the sides of the cake, separating them with red licorice twist "poles." Arrange birthday candles in a circle on the top of the cake. Put one in the center. Let an adult light the candles.

2. Scoop large balls of vanilla ice cream into cupcake liners. Use candies to make clown faces on each. Top each with a sugar cone hat. (Make them ahead of time and keep them in your freezer until you are ready to serve the refreshments.)

More Party Fun:

These games and activities will make your party as much fun as a three-ring circus! Choose which ones to use, depending on the ages of your guests.

- Paint your face (All ages) — Buy face paints or mix up some of your own and create crazy clown faces on your guests. Here's a recipe for face paint: Mix together one teaspoon corn starch and one-half teaspoon cold cream. Add food coloring, a drop at a time. Stir in up to one-half teaspoon water to get the desired consistency. Paint on with a small brush.

● Pin the nose on the clown (Ages 3-5) — Draw a large clown face on a piece of posterboard. Mark an X where the nose should go. Attach double-stick tape or loops of masking tape to large pompoms. (Use a different color for each player, if you wish.) Blindfold players, twirl them around three times, and see who comes the closest to the X.

● Walk the not-so-tight rope (Ages 3-5 and 6-7) — Make a curvy pattern with a rope on the floor. Have everyone line up and try to walk on the rope from one end to the other without stepping off. Take turns laying down the rope in new designs. Older kids can play this as an elimination game. Whoever steps off is out.

● Draw a clown (Ages 6-7) — Give each person a piece of paper and a marker. On the count of three have everyone draw a clown. It's not as easy as it sounds—you have to sit with the paper behind your back and draw without looking! After 60 seconds, hold up the pictures and vote on the funniest.

● Balloon race (Ages 6-7 and 8-10) — Give everyone a balloon. Indicate a start and a finish line. At the signal, race to the finish, keeping your balloon tucked tightly between your knees!

● Balloon burst (Ages 8-10) — This game is best played in a large area. Blow up at least ten balloons in three different colors. Divide into three teams and assign each team a color of balloon. Put the balloons on the floor or ground between the teams. At the starting signal, each team tries to pop the balloons belonging to the other teams. After a couple of minutes, halt the action and count the remaining balloons. The team with the most balloons remaining is the winner.

National Night Out
(First Tuesday in August)

Parents need to teach their children habits that protect them, but they must also be careful not to contribute to a child's insecurities and natural fears by suggesting that danger exists where it does not. This is a fine line that we ask parents to walk and talk. A parent must let the child know that there are threats to personal safety without unduly alarming a child. National Night Out is designed to heighten awareness of crime prevention and to foster police-community partnerships. Knowing the neighborhood is valuable knowledge for a child to possess. The activity of making a map of your community contributes to a child's knowledge. Neighbors can be an "extended family" to a child; it is important to know them. Not all neighbors are well-intentioned. While we don't want to be paranoid, it is important for children to know this, also.

Neighborhood map
(Ages 6-8 and 8-10)

Get a head-start on preventing crime in your neighborhood by getting to know your neighbors. This map activity can help you!

What You'll Need:

➤ plain paper
➤ ruler
➤ markers or crayons

➤ graph paper or roll of shelf paper
➤ pencil

Here's How to Do It:

1. Walk up and down both sides of your street. Take along a pad and pencil and write down house numbers as you pass them. Also write down what color the house is. Note any businesses, parks, schools, and other landmarks in your neighborhood, too.

2. When you get home, transfer your information to a long piece of shelf paper or several sheets of graph paper taped together. Draw a street down the center of the paper. Then draw a house shape for every house on your block. Color the shapes to match the real houses and write the house numbers on the appropriate shape. Add in the other landmarks you noticed.

3. Now it's time to meet the neighbors! With a grown-up's help, plan a block party. It doesn't have to be fancy. Invite everyone on the block to an informal gathering in your front yard. Ask them to bring a snack to share (and maybe a lawn chair or two). Make sure you tell people what time to come. If you want, plan some games for the kids to play.

4. At the party, display your map on a picnic table or card table. Invite people to find their house on the map. Then ask them to write down some information about themselves by their house, such as their names and phone number. Use this information to form a crime watch group on your block. Copies of the map can be made for each household.

5. Use the map and the information you've gathered to form a neighborhood helper's group. Invite neighbors to let one another know when they will be out of town, so others can keep an eye on their house or take in their newspaper or water their gardens. You can also promise to check in on elderly neighbors occasionally, to see if everything is okay with them.

More Family Fun:

● Hold a neighborhood progressive picnic! Arrange to have appetizers at a house at one end of the street, burgers or hotdogs somewhere in the middle, and dessert at the end of the block. Encourage the families from houses not hosting the event to provide the food. Everybody brings their own plates and utensils. (If you live in an apartment building, hold a picnic indoors, moving from apartment to apartment.) It's a great way to get to know your neighbors!

● Contact your local police department for information on crime prevention and National Night Out. Most departments will gladly send you written information or arrange to have an officer come and speak to your neighborhood group.

Friendship Day

(August 6)

*E*verybody likes friends. Braid a bracelet for a friend of yours!

Friendship bracelet
(Ages 6-7 and 8-10)

What You'll Need:

➤ scissors
➤ ruler or tape measure
➤ masking tape
➤ thick yarn, cording, or vinyl braid in three different colors

Here's How to Do It:

1. Cut an 18" long piece from each color of yarn or cord. Tie all three pieces together two inches from one end. Anchor the knot securely to a hard surface, like a table, with masking tape.

2. Hold onto the other ends of the cords. Make a simple braid by passing the left cord over the middle one, making it the new middle cord. Then bring the right cord over the middle, making it the new middle cord. Keep repeating these steps. Try to make your braids even—not too loose or too tight! When you have braided the cord to within two inches of the end opposite the knot, tie the three cords together.

3. Take off the tape and tie the bracelet onto the wrist of a friend!

For younger kids, try this friendship bracelet variation! (Ages 3-5)

What You'll Need:

➤ posterboard
➤ scissors
➤ markers

➤ yarn
➤ paper punch
➤ stick on jewels or stickers (optional)

Here's How to Make It:

1. Cut a strip of poster board, 1/2" to 3/4" wide and long enough to fit loosely around a child's wrist (about five to six inches long).

2. Punch a hole in each end of the strip. Tie a two-inch piece of yarn to each hole.

3. Decorate the strip with markers or stick on jewels or stickers. Tie the yarn ends together to fasten it on a friend's wrist.

More Family Fun:

● Play a friendship game. Form a circle, with one person on the outside. Begin by walking around the circle repeating the words, "Make a new friend, but keep the old. One is silver and the other is gold." Choose someone from the circle to hold hands and walk with you. Repeat the verse, this time letting the person chosen select a friend. Continue until everyone has been chosen. Circle around until the first person is holding the hand of the last. You have made a new circle and can start all over! To add variety to the game, let each new person also choose how to go around the circle. You can skip, hop, run, whatever your want—but you have to hold hands!

● Be a secret pal—do something nice for a friend today, but don't let him or her see you!

September

Activity Book

September Birthday

September 15 through October 15 is National Hispanic Heritage Month. Celebrate your September birthday with a fiesta!

Maraca invitations and party decorations

What You'll Need:

- ➤ construction paper or posterboard
- ➤ rick-rack in two or three colors
- ➤ markers or crayons
- ➤ craft sticks
- ➤ business-size envelopes
- ➤ glue
- ➤ chenille stems (pipe cleaners)

- ➤ scissors
- ➤ 2 paper towel tubes
- ➤ masking tape
- ➤ balloons
- ➤ crepe paper streamers
- ➤ tissue paper

Here's How to Make Them:

1. Invitations: Cut ovals from construction paper or poster board and glue them to craft sticks to make paper maracas. (Make sure they will fit into a business-size envelope.) Glue rick-rack decorations to the front of the maraca and write "What's Shaking?" on the front with a marker. On the back of the maraca write, "A Birthday Fiesta!" and include the party information. Stick the maracas in envelopes and send them off to your guests.

2. Maraca balloon decoration: Blow up and tie two round balloons. Tape each balloon with masking tape to the one end of a paper towel tube. Wrap crepe paper streamers around the base of the balloon to hide the tape. Continue wrapping the tube until you

179

have completely covered it. Hang the maracas over your party table or lay them in the middle as a centerpiece.

3. Tissue paper flowers: You can make these ahead of time or let your guests make their own at the party! Cut 8" squares from tissue paper. Each flower takes six pieces. Pile the squares on top of each other and then fold them together accordian style. Bend the folded strip in the center and wrap a chenille stem tightly around it. Gently pull apart the layers, pulling up toward the center to form a flower.

Mexican serape cake and confetti ice cream

What You'll Need:

- ➤ 9" x 13" cake pan
- ➤ cake mix
- ➤ tray or board or sturdy cardboard big enough to fit the cake
- ➤ aluminum foil
- ➤ vanilla cream frosting
- ➤ black licorice pieces
- ➤ green gel icing in a tube
- ➤ multicolored cake decorating sprinkles
- ➤ yellow food coloring
- ➤ red licorice ropes
- ➤ birthday candles

Here's How to Make It:

1. With a parent helping, bake the cake, following the directions on the package for a single 9" x 13" cake. Remove the cake from the pan and let it cool. Transfer it to a foil-covered tray or board. Add food coloring to the vanilla frosting to make it a bright yellow. Frost the sides and top of the cake, making the frosting as smooth as possible. Use licorice ropes and gel icing to create a patterned border on the two ends of the cake, to resemble a Mexican serape. Use black licorice pieces for a zig-zag pattern, red licorice rope for straight lines, and gel icing for the outside fringe. Arrange your birthday candles in the middle of the cake. Let an adult light them!

2. As you dish up ice cream at the party, sprinkle on multi-colored candy confetti. You can buy a variety of candy sprinkles at the grocery store.

More Party Fun:

Create a lively fiesta with these party games and activities. Choose which ones to play, depending on the ages of your guests.

● Break the piñata! (All ages) — No fiesta would be complete without a piñata! You can buy them in a wide variety of designs at most party goods and discount stores. However, these piñatas can be very hard to break open. For an easy to break piñata you make yourself, turn to page 263. Be sure to pass out paper bags to collect your goodies in!

● Mexican jumping beans (Ages 3-5) — Everyone pretends to be Mexican jumping beans. They jump around whenever they hear music, but they must stop whenever the music does! Turn a lively song cassette on and off several times. Did anyone get mixed up?

● Make-and-take party sashes (Ages 3-5 and 6-7) — Cut a sash from light-colored cloth for each guest. At the party, let them draw on colorful Mexican designs with markers and then tie the sashes around their waists or their heads.

● Make a maraca (Ages 6-7 and 8-10) — Follow the directions on page 114 for making a maraca from papier mâché and an old light bulb. A few days ahead of time, prepare an unpainted maraca for each guest. As they arrive at the party, kids can paint designs on their maraca. The paint should be dry before it's time to go home!

● Enchilada roll (Ages 6-7 and 8-10) — Designate start and finish lines, several yards apart, if possible. (You need a large area for this game!) Line up in two teams of equal size. If you have to, draft a grown-up to make the sides equal. Give each team a towel. At the starting signal, the first person in line rolls up in the towel as an enchilada and continues to roll across the space to the finish line. Once across the finish line, the player runs back and gives the towel to the next person in line. The first team to complete the relay is the winner.

● What's in your chili? (Ages 6-7 and 8-10) — The recipe for this chili is up to your imagination! Sit in a circle. Begin a rhythm by slapping your legs twice and clapping twice. When everyone has joined in, say, "In my chili, there are . . ." and name an ingredient that begins with the letter A. Then pass the play to another person by asking, "What's in (person's name) chili?" The person named repeats "In my chili there are . . ." and adds an ingredient that starts with B. Then he or she passes the play on to another person. Continue until everyone has had a chance to name an ingredient or go through the entire alphabet!

Labor Day

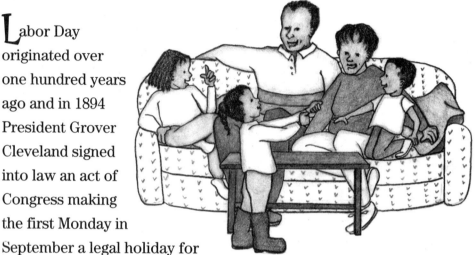

Labor Day originated over one hundred years ago and in 1894 President Grover Cleveland signed into law an act of Congress making the first Monday in September a legal holiday for federal employees. It has since become a universally observed holiday in the United States and Canada. It is a good day to speak to children about work. Just what is it that Daddy and Mommy do when they go to work or work at home? Children like to "pretend" they will be such and such when they grow up. It is useful to encourage this imaginative play process. It is also useful, if possible, to bring a child to your workplace occasionally. This removes some of the "mystery" about what a parent does in those hours away from home each day. It can help a child to appreciate the hard work a parent undertakes to provide security and comfort for the family.

Play "What's My Job?"

(All ages)

What You'll Need:

➤ at least two people
   (but the more the better!)

➤ paper and pencil
➤ bowl or basket

Here's How to Play:

1. Talk about some different occupations before you start. What's the most unusual job you can think of? Write down a number of occupations on pieces of paper and put the in a bowl or basket.

2. Divide into two teams of equal size (or close to equal).

3. The first team draws a slip from the bowl and then gets a minute to decide who will do the acting. They then act out their occupation for the opposing team. If the opposing team can guess correctly within three minutes they score a point. If they can't, the other team scores.

4. Teams take turns drawing slips until all have been used. The team with the most points wins.

5. For younger players, play a simpler version of the game: Let individuals think up an occupation and act it out for the rest of the group. The first person to guess the job correctly gets to act out next. Don't keep score—just play as long as you want!

185

More Family Fun:

● Talk about what the grown-ups in the family do for a living. If possible, arrange to visit their workplaces.

● Make a family job chart. Assign tasks to every family member and check them off as they are completed. Plan a special outing or treat when everyone gets the job done!

● Visit the library and check out books on different occupations. Read them together. Then have everyone draw a picture of what they wish they could be—grown-ups included!

National Grandparent's Day

(first Sunday in September after Labor Day)

With our system of interstate highways and jet airplanes, America has become a very mobile society. We leave our birthplace to go to college, to look for work, to join a spouse. This can be very exciting but has its disadvantages, especially for children. The extended family of grandparents, aunts, uncles, and cousins can be a resource for families in helping to nurture children. The warm relationships that accrue from such close contact can be a very

187

positive influence on children. Even if grandparents are not close by, children should be encouraged to stay in contact. The activities suggested below will foster this contact; I am certain you can think of many other ways to add to that potentially great grandparent-child relationship.

Do your grandparents live far from you? Send a long distance hug! (Ages 3-5)

What You'll Need:

- ➤ shelf paper
- ➤ construction paper
- ➤ lightweight fabric scraps or gift wrap
- ➤ markers or crayons
- ➤ tape
- ➤ scissors
- ➤ glue
- ➤ large manila envelope
- ➤ Velcro self-adhesive fastener

Here's How You Do It:

1. Tear off three pieces of shelf paper, a little longer than you are tall. Tape the pieces together to make one wide sheet.

2. Lie on your back on the paper and spread your arms out wide. Have someone trace around your whole body. Try not to wiggle!

3. Cut out the shape. Then use markers or crayons to draw on eyes and a nose and a mouth. Color on hair or cut some from construction paper and glue it on. Glue on clothes you cut from cloth or paper. If you want, you can dress and decorate the backside too. Does it look like you?

4. Attach one side of the self-adhering Velcro fastener to the front of one paper hand and the other Velcro fastener to the back of the other hand. Now your paper person can give a hug!

5. Fold up the paper person and mail it to your grandparents in a large envelope. Add a note that says, "I can't be there, but I've sent a hug! Wrap this around you whenever you miss me!"

Make an extra special edition greeting for Grandparents' Day!
(Ages 6-7 and 8-9)

What You'll Need:

➤ paper

➤ pencil

➤ tape recorder (optional)

➤ newspaper

➤ markers

➤ scissors

➤ glue

Here's How to Do It:

1. Be a newspaper, radio, or TV reporter. Make a list of questions to ask your grandparent, such as:
- When were you born? Where?
- Have your always lived in the same place?
- What games did you like to play when you were young?
- Who was your favorite teacher? Why?
- What subject did you like best in school? What did you like least?
- What are your hobbies?

2. Arrange to visit or call your grandparent for an interview. Ask the questions you've prepared, and write down the answers. If you have tape recorder, you could tape the conversation, but ask if it's okay with your grandparent first.

3. Use the information you've gathered to write a news story about your grandparent! Write or type it on plain paper. Then paste the paper onto the front page of an old newspaper, to make it seem like one of the real stories. Cover up the headline for the day by gluing a piece of plain paper over it. Use a marker to write a new headline, HAPPY GRANDPARENTS' DAY! in large letters.
Sign your name somewhere on the paper.

4. Mail or deliver the card to your grandparent with love. Say thanks for sharing some time and memories together!

More Family Fun:

- If your grandparent lives a distance away, keep in touch through the mail. Write letters on the backs of art projects you've done in school, send them postcards when you are traveling, or complete a cooperative crossword puzzle—send it back and forth, each adding a word until you're done!

Grandma Moses Day
(September 7)

Grandma Moses taught herself how to paint when she was 78 years old! Take inspiration from her and paint something today.

Spin a color painting game (Ages 3-5 and 6-7)

What You'll Need:

- red, yellow, and blue paint
- paint brushes (one for each color)
- paint smock (an old shirt worn backwards will do!)
- large pieces of paper
- bottle suitable for spinning
- newspaper
- 6 paper plates

Here's How to Do It:

1. Before playing, paint the centers of two paper plates red, blue, and yellow. When the paint is dry, arrange the plates in a circle on the floor in this pattern: red, blue, yellow, red, blue, yellow. Have the edges of the plates touch. Put a bottle in the middle of the circle.

2. Set up your paints, brushes, and paper. (Cover your table with newspaper first!) Put on your smock.

3. Take turns spinning the bottle. Call out the color it points to. Then paint a picture of as many things as you can think of that are the same color. For instance, if it points to yellow, you can paint a sun, a banana, a chick, and a taxi! How many pictures can you paint?

More Family Fun:

Try these ideas to stimulate your artistic juices:

● Look closely at a flower petal or feather or piece of wood and draw the lines and shapes you see.

● Cut a picture of a face from a magazine. Glue half of it to a piece of paper. Draw or paint the other half. Or glue cut-outs of houses to a piece of shelf paper and paint on figures and trees and other details.

● Turn a photograph upside down and paint or draw what you see.

● Practice blind contour drawing—drawings made without looking at your paper!

● Paint a picture with something besides a brush. Try a feather or a weed or a sponge—or your fingers!

● Visit an art gallery or museum or check out a book about Grandma Moses from your library.

American Indian Day

Several states honor Native Americans on different days throughout the year. In Oklahoma, American Indian Day is observed on the first Saturday following the full moon in September. The day is marked by powwows and other festivities that reflect the heritage of these first Americans.

Make a totem to honor the tribes of the Northwest (Ages 3-5)

What You'll Need:

➤ four or five large coffee cans with plastic lids

➤ four or five pieces of construction paper in different colors

➤ posterboard or light-weight cardboard

➤ crayons or markers

➤ scissors

➤ transparent tape and masking tape

Here's How to Do It:

1. Cut each piece of construction paper so that it fits around a coffee can. Draw a different face on each piece. (You might look in an encyclopedia or book about American Indian tribes of the Northwest to see what some actual totems look like.)

2. Wrap the construction paper around the coffee cans and secure them with tape.

3. Cut two eagle wing shapes from posterboard and tape them to the sides of one coffee can.

4. Stack up the coffee cans to make the totem. Put the winged one at the top. Tape the cans together with masking tape.

Try your hand at weaving like the Native Americans of the Southwest

(Ages 6-7 and 8-10)

What You'll Need:

➤ foam food tray

➤ yarn

➤ ruler

➤ scissors

Here's How to Do It:

1. Make a loom by cutting slits every half inch along the top and bottom edges of the foam tray. Make sure you have the same number of slits on each end.

2. Wrap yarn around the front and back of the tray, passing it through the slits on the ends. Keep the yarn taut, but don't wrap too tightly, or the tray will break!

3. Starting on the left edge, weave yarn over and under the yarn on the front side of the loom. When you get to the right edge, turn around and go back the other way. If you want, try using different colors of yarn to make a pattern. Just tie the new color onto the end of your yarn when you want to change. You might try weaving other things into your design, like feathers or grasses or twigs.

4. When you are done, cut the yarn on the back of the loom and carefully remove the weaving. You can tie the long pieces of yarn together in clumps of three for a fringe.

More Family Fun:

● The 1.5 million Native Americans living in the United States today belong to many different tribes, each with its own traditions. Investigate the customs of Native American tribes who live or may have once lived in your area. You can find out information through local and state historical societies or through Native American cultural institutes.

● Not all Indians lived in tepees. Older kids might like to build scale models of different kinds of Native American dwellings. Tepees, earth lodges, and adobe houses are some shelters. Visit your library to find out more!

● Check out some books of traditional Native American legends and folktales. Your local or school library should have a list of some.

Holiday Fun

October

Activity Book

October Birthday

Turn your October birthday into a fall festival!

Leaf invitations and hayride table decorations

What You'll Need:

➤orange and yellow construction paper ➤envelopes

➤markers ➤scissors

➤cardboard box, about 8″ x 10″ ➤cardboard scraps

➤toy horse or tractor ➤Shredded Wheat biscuits

Here's How to Make Them:

1. Invitations: Cut leaf shapes from construction paper. On the front of each leaf write, "Dropping by to invite you to a party!" On the back, write your party information. Slip them into the envelopes and mail them.

2. Hayride centerpiece: Cut down the sides of the cardboard box to about an inch. Glue on four cardboard wheels. Hook up a toy horse or a toy tractor to the box. Crumble Shredded Wheat cereal into the box for hay. Arrange your pumpkin cupcakes on top of the hay.

Pumpkin spice cupcakes

What You'll Need:

➤spice cake mix
➤paper cupcake
liners (orange, if
possible)
➤cream cheese
ready-to-serve
frosting
➤red and yellow food coloring
➤pumpkin shaped candies
➤birthday candles

Here's How to Do It:

1. With a parent helping, follow the directions on the package for baking the cupcakes. Allow them to cool before frosting them.

2. Tint the cream cheese frosting orange by stirring in red and yellow food coloring a drop at a time until you get the desired color. Frost the tops of the cupcakes. Put a candy pumpkin or a birthday candle in the center of each.

More Party Fun:

Entertain your guests with these games and activities. Select which ones to use depending on the ages of the kids you invite.

● Leaf adventures (All ages) — Rake big piles of leaves in your yard or a park. Hide things like Frisbees or balls or other outdoor toys in the piles. Let the kids dig through the leaves to find the items, and then use the toys for free play. You can also create a maze from the leaves and see how fast kids can find their way through. You might just want to jump in the piles. Enjoy a great autumn day!

● Outdoor fun (All ages) — Go apple picking or pumpkin picking if you live near an orchard or farm. Many such places offer free hay rides this time of year. Or visit a nearby nature center to find out what happens in the fall. After the excursion, go back to your house for cake.

● Make leaf art (Ages 3-5 and 6-7) — Collect some leaves and glue them to a piece of construction paper. Draw a picture around each leaf. You can make people or animals or anything!

● Peter Pumpkin (Ages 3-5 and 6-7) — Play an autumn version of "Simon Says." Let kids take turns being Peter Pumpkin and giving commands. Remember—only move when "Peter Pumpkin" says so or you'll be out!

● Stuff a scarecrow (Ages 6-7 and 8-10) — Before the party, make two scarecrow bodies by attaching old shirts to pairs of old pants. Tie the sleeves and legs shut. (You can pick up the old clothes at a garage sale.) At the party, divide into two teams. Give each team a pile of newspapers. At the starting signal, the teams begin crumpling up the newspaper and stuffing the scarecrow. The first team to finish, wins. (You can make heads for your scarecrows by stuffing old pillow cases or paper bags and drawing faces on them.)

● Party pumpkins (Ages 6-7 and 8-10) — Paint faces on mini pumpkins for fun take-home favors. Use acrylic paints—they are easy to work with and they dry quickly.

● Pumpkin patch word game (Ages 8-10) — Give each player a piece of paper and a pencil. Have them write down the words they can make from letters in PUMPKIN PATCH. Set a timer for a minute or two. Who came up with the longest list?

Child Health Day
(October 2)

Child Health Day has been in existence since 1928. It is a good day to have some conversation with your child about what they can do to maintain good health. Touch on such subjects as food, sleep, and exercise. It is important to make a child realize, early in life, that they are in charge. They control what happens to them by their attitude toward health matters. This is a lesson that brings life-long dividends.

Play "Where Does It Hurt?" (Ages 3-5)

What You'll Need:

➤ at least two people

Here's How to Play:

1. Choose one person to be the doctor. The rest of the players are the patients.

2. The doctor begins by asking, "Where does it hurt?" Then the doctor names different parts on the body, like "Your ear? Your nose? Your kncccap? Your elbow?" while the patients point to that place. The doctor starts out slowly and gets faster and faster until the patients can't keep up anymore. When the patients fall down laughing, it's time to choose another doctor!

Assemble a first aid kit
(Ages 6-7 and 8-10)

What You'll Need:

- box with a lid (a plastic container with a snap-on lid is ideal!)
- adhesive bandages
- tweezers
- first aid cream
- first aid tape
- scissors
- thermometer
- gauze
- antiseptic wipes
- non-aspirin pain relievers
- puffy paints (optional)

Here's How to Do It:

1. Gather the necessary items. If you need to, plan a trip to the drugstore.

2. If you wish, you can paint first aid symbols, like a red cross or bandages, on the lid or sides of the box with puffy paint.

3. As you arrange the items in the box, talk about what each is used for. *Remember that these items are not toys and only grown-ups can handle medicines!*

4. Put the first aid kit in a convenient place, but out of the way of little children. It's a good idea to carry a kit in your car, especially when you are going on a trip!

More Family Fun:

● Take out your play doctor kit and set up a hospital. You can treat sick dolls and stuffed animals and family members. Take turns being the doctor and the patient.

● Check out some books about doctors and dentists. Take a tour of a local hospital. Visit a doctor's office or dentist's office regularly.

● Talk about what you can do to keep healthy. What exercise do you get? Do you eat the right foods? Plan a healthy meal together and take a walk afterward.

● Put on some lively music for a family aerobic workout!

● Check your house to make sure it's safe. Are there safety plugs in outlets? Do you have a working smoke detector? Are medicines kept out of kids' reach? Do you know what to do in case of an emergency? Dial 911!

Columbus Day

(Second Monday in October)

Columbus Day is officially October 12, but in the United States it is celebrated on the second Monday in October. The day commemorates the arrival of Christopher Columbus to North America on October 12, 1492. It was first celebrated in 1792 in the states of New York and Maryland. Today it is a federal holiday, and a time to reflect on the adventuresome spirit of early explorers like Columbus.

Make Columbus's ships from bars of soap!

(Ages 3-5 and 6-7)

What You'll Need:

➤three bars of soap that will float

➤construction paper

➤markers

➤bamboo skewers

➤table knife

➤scissors

Here's How to Make Them:

1. Cut the construction paper into nine squares to make sails. Color on the sails however you wish. You could print on the names of Columbus's ships: *The Niña, The Pinta,* and *The Santa Maria.*

2. Let a grown-up help you cut a little off the corners on each bar of soap. (Save the soap pieces and add them to some water in a bottle to make liquid soap!)

3. Have a grown-up cut the skewers down to six inches. Then push the pointed end of the skewer through the construction paper sail near the top and bottom and stick the skewer into the bar of soap. Put three sails on each bar of soap.

4. You're ready to sail off to discover new worlds in your bathtub! Just blow on the sails!

More Family Fun:

● Investigate how early explorers found their way across uncharted oceans. Visit a planetarium to learn more about traveling by reading the stars, or check out a book on sea navigation. Learn how a compass works.

● Among Spanish-speaking Americans, Columbus Day is known as El Dia de la Raza or the Day of the Race. This name recalls how Spanish people who settled the islands Columbus landed on inter-married with the Indians who lived there. Later, Africans who were brought to the area intermarried with both the Spanish and the Indians. Their descendants celebrate this unique culture with colorful parades and fiestas. Why not observe Columbus Day fiesta style?

United Nations Day

(October 24)

Celebrate the different countries around the world!

Create a "small world" tree (Ages 6-7 and 8-10)

What You'll Need:

- a coffee can
- atlas or encyclopedia that shows flags of the world
- dead tree branch
- crayons or markers

- white, blue, and green construction paper
- plaster of paris
- yarn or string
- transparent tape or glue

Here's How to Make It:

1. Cover the coffee can with blue paper. Look in your atlas for a world map. Use it to cut out land shapes from green paper and glue them onto the blue paper. Your can will look something like a map!

2. Fill the coffee can half-way with a plaster of paris mixture, and anchor the tree branch in it. Follow the directions on the plaster package for correct mixing. Do not dump extra plaster down your drain. It can harden and wreck your plumbing! When the plaster is hard, you're ready to add decorations.

3. Draw and color tiny flags of many nations. Use the flag pictures in your atlas or encyclopedia as a guide. Cut out the flags and glue or tape them to yarn or string to make a garland. Hang the garland on your branch.

4. Add other decorations you may have to represent different countries: little dolls or figures, foreign coins glued to cardboard circles, candies or cookies, jewelry—whatever!

5. As a finishing touch, cut a dove from white paper and hang it on the tree. The dove reminds us of the United Nations mission to promote peace throughout the world.

More Family Fun:

● Host a "Round the World" party. Invite friends to come dressed in costumes from many nations. Serve a buffet of foods from around the world or choose one country's cuisine to highlight. Play recordings of international music that you borrow from the library. Try a few games from other countries or tell stories from different lands. Use your "Small World" tree as a centerpiece on your table. You could tie on little party favors for your guests to take home.

● Learn more about the United Nations. Read about it in an encyclopedia. If you live near New York City or plan to visit it sometime, take a tour of the United Nations Building while you're there.

Halloween
(October 31)

Halloween is certainly one of the principle children's events in any year. Much has been said about Halloween safety but the message bears repeating.

- Check on costumes to be certain they are flame-proof, fire-retardant.
- Eyes should never be covered with a mask that makes it impossible to use our eyes in crossing streets.
- Young children should always be accompanied by an adult.
- Candy or fruit should not be eaten until checked by an adult.

You can probably think of some other safety rules you want to impose. Don't be shy. Halloween can be fun but it can also be dangerous. "Trick or Treat" is a phrase with a nice ring to it but children should understand that this is not a day when we do things that cause suffering to people.

Halloween is a favorite holiday for kids. What could be more fun than dressing up in costumes and getting candy? How about some games to play after trick-or-treating or during your Halloween party?

Boo Bingo (Ages 3-5)

What You'll Need:

➤plain paper

➤candy corn

➤pencil or pen

➤bowl

Here's How to Do It:

1. Prepare Bingo cards ahead of time. Draw a large grid with nine squares. In each square, draw a simple Halloween picture: a cat, a bat, a witch's hat, a ghost, a broom, a jack-o-lantern, a spider, a full moon, and candy corn. Make a bingo card for each player, but vary the order in which you draw the pictures, so that everyone's card is not identical! Draw an extra set of pictures and cut them apart. Put them in a bowl.

2. Give everyone a card and some candy corn for markers. Take turns drawing a slip from the bowl and calling out what is pictured. Cover that picture on your card. The first person to cover three pictures in a row (across, down, or diagonally) and yells "BOO!" is the winner.

Toss a ghost (Ages 3-5 and 6-7)

What You'll Need:

➤small plastic sandwich bags with twist ties
➤white paper towels
➤rice
➤1/4 cup measure
➤string
➤black marker
➤three plastic buckets or large coffee cans

Here's How to Do It:

1. Pour a quarter cup of rice into a plastic sandwich bag. Twist the bag tightly around the rice and wrap it securely with a twist tie so the rice cannot escape. Tie a paper towel around the rice end of the bag with string. Draw a ghost face with black marker on the towel.

2. Make three more ghosts.

3. Set up the three buckets or cans opposite the players. Put the first container four feet away, the second five feet, and the third six feet from the players.

4. Take turns tossing the four ghosts. If a ghost lands in the first container, you get 5 points. If one lands in the second container, you get 10 points. The third container is worth 20 points. The person with the highest score wins.

The witch's cauldron
(Ages 6-7 and 8-10)

What You'll Need:

➤several players (the more, the better!)

Here's How to Play:

1. Sit in a circle. One person begins by saying, "I am the witch, and in my cauldron I put . . ." and names some ghoulish item to drop in the cauldron.

2. The person to the left then repeats what the first person said and adds an item of his or her own. Continue around the circle adding creepy ingredients as you go. But watch out! If you forget an item or name them in the wrong order, you're out! The last person left in the circle wins.

More Family Fun:

● Make waiting to eat your Halloween goodies fun! When you get home, dump your candy out and play a sorting game. All chocolate goes in one pile, gum in another, and so on. Or you can sort them by the colors on the wrappers. Kids who can read can sort them by the names on the wrappers. While you sort, a grown-up can check to see if all the treats are safe to eat. Remember, always wait until you get home before eating any candy!

● Instead of going trick-or-treating this year, how about just treating? Dress up in your costumes and visit a local hospital or nursing home or care center. Go from room to room passing out treats, such as candy or stickers. Have a grown-up contact the hospital or center before you go, to find out about its visitors' policies and what treats are appropriate.

Diwali
(Hindu Festival of Light)

This holiday usually falls in October or November. Diwali means "a row of lights." It is a celebration of light over darkness. Hindu people light divas (lamps) in honor of Lakshi, the goddess of fortune and wealth. In the evening, girls float their divas across the river. If the lights make it across, the girl's family is assured of good fortune in the year to come.

Make a clay diva
(Ages 6-7 and 8-10)

What You'll Need

➤1 cup salt
➤4 cups flour
➤1¹/2 cups warm water
➤spoon

➤large mixing bowl
➤acrylic paints
➤paint brush
➤votive candle

Here's How to Do It:

1. Make baker's clay with this recipe:
Dissolve the salt in warm water. Let the mixture cool. Then add the flour and knead for 10 minutes.

2. Roll a handful of clay into a ball. Press your thumb into the ball and turn the ball between your fingers until you have formed a bowl big enough to hold a votive candle. Don't make the sides too thin or they will flop over. Pinch one side of your bowl to make a lip, like on a pitcher. You have formed a diva! Press the diva onto your table to make sure the bottom is flat.

3. Let a grown-up bake the diva in a 300°F oven for about an hour to harden it.

4. When the diva has cooled, you can paint colorful designs on the outside. Put your candle in the diva. A grown-up can light the candle for you. Remember—do not leave the candle burning unattended and do not touch it while it is lit!

More Family Fun:

● Visit your library and check out some books about India or the Hindu religion. What are some other holidays they celebrate? What other religions do many people in India practice?

Holiday Fun

November

Activity Book

November Birthday

B last off to adventure, and celebrate your birthday in space! Make intergalactic invitations and rocket party favors. Hang stellar decorations, and plan some games that will send your guests into orbit. Here's how!

Space invitations and decorations

What You'll Need:

- construction paper
- envelopes
- dark blue paper tablecloth
- stick-on foil stars (gold or silver)
- toilet paper tubes
- toy spaceships (optional)
- tissue paper or crepe paper
- tape or glue
- markers
- scissors

Here's How to Make Them:

1. Invitations: Cut rocket ships from construction paper and write "Blast off to Birthday Fun!" on them. Add your party information, then stick them in envelopes and send.

2. Rocket party favors: Let guests make their own rockets by gluing or taping construction paper tail pieces and nose cones to paper tubes. Draw on other details with markers. Cut streamers from tissue or crepe paper and attach to the ends of the rockets. You're ready to blast-off!

3. Table decorations: Stick foil stars all over a dark blue paper tablecloth. Cut planet shapes from construction paper and tape them to the tablecloth, too. If you have any toy spaceships, put them in the middle of the table.

Galaxy cake and meteor mix balls

What You'll Need:

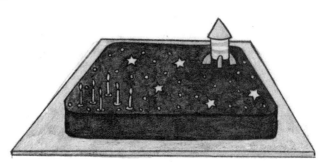

➤cake mix

➤9" x 13" pan

➤aluminum foil

➤chocolate fudge (dark) frosting

➤silver cake decorating beads

➤small plastic spaceship

➤birthday candles

➤board, tray, or sturdy cardboard to fit cake

➤margarine

➤waxed paper

➤Rice Krispies cereal

➤star-shaped breakfast cereal

➤Kix cereal

➤marshmallows

➤2-3 quart saucepan

➤ice cream scoop

Here's How to Make Them:

1. Galaxy cake: Bake the cake, following the directions on the package for a 9" x 13" single layer. With a parent's help, remove the cake from the pan and let it cool completely. Transfer it to a foil-covered tray or board. Frost the top and sides of the cake with fudge frosting (the darker the color, the better). Sprinkle on silver

226

decorating beads for stars. Add a few star-shaped cereal pieces. Place the toy spaceship on one side of the cake and arrange the birthday candles on the other.

2. Meteor mix balls: Melt 1/4 cup margarine in a large saucepan over a low heat. Add one bag of marshmallows and stir until melted. Remove from heat and stir in 2 cups Rice Krispies, 2 cups Kix cereal, and 2 cups star-shaped cereal. Mix well. Shape into two-inch balls, using an ice cream scoop or waxed paper to protect your hands.

More Party Fun:

Make your party really "out of this world" with these games and activities. Select which to use, based on the ages of your guests.

- Be stargazers (Ages 3-5) — Give each guest a paper cup and a pencil. Have them poke holes in the bottom of the cup to make stars (a grown-up can help little kids). Turn off the lights and draw the shades to make the room dark. Take turns putting the cups over the end of a flashlight and shining the stars on the ceiling. (Having a flashlight for every person is even more fun!)

- Catch a falling star (Ages 3-5 and 6-7) — Cut stars from construction paper. (Tracing around a star-shaped cookie cutter makes it easy.) Cut at least six stars for every guest. Put all the stars in the middle of a sheet. Have everyone grab hold of the sheet and on the count of three, toss the stars high in the air. Drop the sheet and scramble to pick of the stars. Who got the most? Repeat the game as many times as you want.

● Alien race (Ages 6-7) — Hang a long piece of shelf paper on the wall at kid's height. Blindfold each person and give each a marker or crayon. Set a timer for 15 seconds. Have everyone draw a picture of an alien on the shelf paper. When the timer goes off, remove the blindfolds and laugh at your pictures!

● Navigate the planets (Ages 6-7) — Tie long strings onto several balloons and hang them from the ceiling as an obstacle course. (They should hang down to the heads of the kids.). Clear away any furniture or other objects from the course. Have the group form pairs of players. Blindfold one person in each pair. Teams take turns navigating the course, letting the player who is not blindfolded give voice directions only to the one who is. Whichever team gets through with the fewest planet collisions, wins. Play twice, to give everyone a chance to be blindfolded.

● Sail a ship through the worm hole (Ages 8-10) — Play this game outdoors (or use a foam flying disk or paper airplane indoors). Hang a hula hoop from a tree (or the ceiling). This is the worm hole. Stand several feet away, and take turns trying to fly a Frisbee (or foam disk or paper airplane) through the hoop. Give each person three tries. The one who makes the most, wins. (To make the game more challenging, give the hoop a little push!)

● Mixed-up solar system (Ages 8-10) — For each player, make a list of jumbled planet names:

1. cumerry
2. otlup
3. tunnepe
4. retujpi
5. reaht
6. suven
7. srma
8. trasun
9. sunrau

The first person to unscramble all the names is the winner.

● Extra-terrestrial fun (All ages) — If you live near a planetarium, spend part of your party there! Older kids might enjoy a sleep-over party—rent space movies, use a telescope to check out the stars at night, or read stories about space adventures.

National Author's Day
(November 1)

This holiday originated with the General Federation of Women's Clubs way back in 1929. Its intent was to recognize the contributions made by authors to American literature and their strengthening of our nation. It is a wonderful thing to encourage a young person who enjoys using words and enjoys placing them on paper. This usually comes about when a child is introduced to the pleasures of reading at a young age and when the imagination of that child is encouraged to develop. Imagination is a wonderful tool for a human being and leads to accomplishments in all fields of endeavor, from the arts to the sciences. Doctors, lawyers, bankers, and businesspeople all use imagination. Encouraging a child to write and encouraging the development of imagination will serve a child throughout life.

Build a story (Ages 6-7 and 8-10)

What You'll Need:

➤ paper
➤ markers or crayons

➤ pencil
➤ stapler

Here's How to Do It:

1. One person starts by writing an opening sentence for a story at the top of the paper. Then the paper is passed to the next person who adds a line and passes it on to the next person. Continue passing the paper around until it comes back to the first person again. (Older players can write down the words for younger players.)

2. Read your story out loud. Does it make sense?

3. Now divide up the story and have people draw pictures to accompany the words. Assemble the pages, add a front and back cover, and staple them together into a book.

More Family Fun:

- Go to the library and check out several books by a favorite author. Or pick some books by an author you have never heard of.

- Write a letter to your favorite author, telling why you like his or her books. You can write to an author through the publisher of the book. The publisher's address is usually printed on the copyright page.

- Do you want to be an author when you get older? Start writing in a journal now. Record what goes on in your life. Who knows, maybe you'll turn it into a best-seller someday!

Sandwich Day
(November 3)

Now, here is a silly holiday and one that can be lots of fun. Today is the anniversary of the birth of the fourth Earl of Sandwich. He lived over two hundred years ago and is credited as the inventor of the sandwich. Guess who Captain Cook named the Sandwich Islands after? Here is an idea for making a super sub sandwich.

See if you can dream up a really silly sandwich. Try to guess how many sandwiches each family member eats in a year. What a silly holiday!

Make a super sub sandwich! (All ages)

What You'll Need:

➤one or two loaves of French bread

➤butter, mustard, mayonnaise, or your favorite spread

➤assorted sandwich fillers—cheese, sliced meat, egg salad, tuna—it's up to you!

➤veggies—lettuce, sprouts, cucumbers, onions, tomatoes

➤sharp knife

➤butter knife

➤plates for the ingredients

Here's How to Do It:

1. Let a grown-up use the sharp knife to slice the vegetables, cheese, and other stuff that might need cutting. Kids can wash lettuce and pile ingredients on separate plates. Make sure everyone washes their hands first!

2. Slice the top off the loaf of bread and place the loaf on a table or counter where everyone can reach it. Give each person a plate of ingredients, line up in the order you want the ingredients added (butter first, onions last?), and start layering it on. If you have more plates of ingredients than you have people, just take another turn on the assembly line until everything is piled on the sandwich.

3. If your group likes to sing, try these words to the tune of "This Is the Way We Wash Our Clothes," as you add each layer:

This is the way we build our sub,

build our sub, build our sub

this is the way we build our sub

on Earl of Sandwich Day!

Other verses could start:

This is the way we butter our bread...

This is the way we pile on cheese...

This is the way we add the meat...

This is the way we gobble our sub...

Get the idea? Just adapt the words to match your ingredients. When you're done building, put on the top and slice off chunks for everybody. Happy eating!

More Family Fun:

● Bite into a good book. Kids will love the humorous book, *Sam's Sandwich*, by David Pelham (Dutton Children's Books, 1991). It looks just like a sandwich!

After reading it, you might try making one of your own.

● Serve sandwiches for every meal today!

Election Day

(First Tuesday after the first Monday in November)

No one is too young to vote in a family election!

Hold a family election

(Ages 6-7 and 8-10)

What You'll Need:

➤posterboard
➤paper
➤box with a lid

➤markers
➤pencils

Here's How to Do It:

1. Make a list of offices to run for. You might include the traditional offices of President and Vice President, or you may want to invent some new ones. How about Director of Saturday Morning Activities or Chief Meal Planner or Vice President of Who Sits Where in the Car?

2. Once you have decided on some offices, have everyone choose what they want to try running for.

3. Make campaign posters and put them up around the house. Plan a time for candidates to give speeches on why people should vote for them. Urge everyone to get out and vote.

4. Cut a hole in the lid of a box for a ballot box. Prepare paper ballots. Write down each office and underneath it, write the names of the people who are running. Draw boxes beside each name. Make a ballot for each person in your family. To vote for someone, you will put an X in the box by his or her name.

5. After marking your ballot, stick it in the ballot box. When all have voted, open the box and count the ballots. Who won?

More Family Fun:

Families with school-age kids might observe Election Day with these ideas:

● Find out more about your government. If you have the chance, take a tour of your capitol or assembly house and see your representatives in action. Check out books about government and how laws are made.

● Predict who you think will win in elections this year. Then watch the election returns on television. Did your candidates win? Were you surprised?

● Visit a polling place today. Do people vote on paper ballots or by machine? Ask the election judges if voter turnout is heavy or light. What are some things that encourage people to vote today? What could discourage them?

Thanksgiving Day

W hen the Pilgrims settled in what is now the Commonwealth of Massachusetts way back in 1620, they were settling a wilderness. Ask your child to imagine a place with woods and cold weather, deep snows and winds and no supermarkets or other stores to buy food and clothing. It was a very rough first winter, but most of the

Pilgrims survived with great help from the friendly Native Americans. The Pilgrims and the Native Americans gathered in the autumn of 1621 to give thanks for their survival. This is a very American holiday and the symbol—the turkey—is a very American bird. Thanksgiving is a day when extended family and friends come together with warm feelings and in thanksgiving. Try to convey to your child how fortunate we are and how thankful we should be.

Create some napkin rings for your holiday table
(Ages 3-5)

What You'll Need:

➤paper towel tubes   ➤scissors
➤dried beans, macaroni, or Indian corn
➤paint   ➤newspaper
➤paint brush   ➤glue

Here's How to Make Them:

1. Have a grown-up cut the paper tube into one-inch rings.

2. Cover your work space with newspaper. Paint outside and inside the rings. Let the paint dry.

3. Glue on colorful beans, Indian corn, or macaroni in whatever design you like. If you want, skip the painting and cover the whole ring with Indian corn or beans!

Make a pinecone turkey decoration (Ages 6-7)

What You'll Need:

➤pinecone

➤markers or crayons

➤glue

➤construction paper in a variety of colors

➤scissors

Here's How to Make It:

1. Cut bright colors of construction paper into strips about three inches long and one inch wide. You will need 10 strips for each turkey. Trim the strips so that they are a little thinner at the bottom than they are at the top. Color on feather designs, if you wish.

2. Cut out a turkey head from light brown construction paper. Color an eye on each side and add a red wattle (the wiggly skin on a turkey's chin).

3. Set the pinecone on its side. Glue the turkey head close to the pointed end of the cone. Then dip the narrow ends of the strips in glue and stick them, fan-style into the pinecone near the flat end to make the tail.

Design a "thankful" table runner (Ages 8-10)

What You'll Need:

➤a piece of plain light-colored cotton, 18" x 36"
➤orange, green, yellow, and brown fabric paints
➤pencil
➤newspaper

Here's How to Do It:

1. Have a grown-up stitch a narrow hem around all four sides of the runner. If you don't have a sewing machine, you can create a fringed edge by pulling off a half inch of threads on all sides. (Make sure your fabric is cut straight on the grain. If it isn't, your fringe will be crooked.)

2. Have family members take turns writing down things they are thankful for along the outside edge of the runner. Write fairly large in pencil first. Older kids or grown-ups can write down what younger kids say, or younger children can draw a picture of something they are thankful for. Put the person's name after his or her contribution. Keep adding things until you have gone all around the outside edge.

3. Place the runner on newspaper. Carefully go over the writing with fabric paint, changing colors from name to name. If you want, paint some fall designs such as leaves and pumpkins in the center of the runner. Let the paint dry completely. Use the runner on your Thanksgiving Day table!

More Family Fun:

● Check out a book from the library about the first Thanksgiving and read it together while you wait for the turkey to get done.

● Hold a fall scavenger hunt after dinner. Do it in your backyard or a park. Divide into teams, give each a small bag, and go looking for things such as an acorn, a maple leaf, a pinecone, a twig in the shape of a letter of the alphabet (not counting I!), and a speckled stone. The first team to collect all the items gets a second piece of pumpkin pie!

World Hello Day

(November 21)

T ake time today to exchange hellos with a friend!

Make a string telephone
(Ages 3-5)

What You'll Need:

➤ 2 paper cups

➤ string

➤ scissors

Here's How to Make It:

1. Cut a long piece of string.

2. Punch a little hole in the bottom of each cup. Push one end of the string through each hole to connect the cups. Tie a big knot on each end so the string won't slip out.

3. To say hello to your friend, pull the string tight and talk into one cup while your friend listens in the other. Take turns talking and listening.

Send a friendly hello with an accordion card
(Ages 6-7 and 8-10)

What You'll Need:

➤plain paper   ➤scissors

➤tape   ➤business-size envelope

➤crayons or markers

Here's How to Make It:

1. Tape two or three pieces of paper together end to end to make one long sheet.

2. Fold the long sheet accordion style so that it will fit into the envelope.

3. Write a different "Hello" on each of the folds on the card. When you get to the bottom, turn the card over and do the other side! Here are some different ways to say hello to get you started:

- Aloha (ah-LO-ha)—Hawaiian
- Hola (OH-la)—Spanish
- Shalom (shah-LOME)—Hebrew
- Wei (way)—Chinese
- Bonjour (bon-ZHOOR)—French
- Jambo (JAHM-bo)—Swahili
- Salaam (sah-LAHM)—Arabic
- Güten Tag (GU-ten TAHG)—German
- Konnichiwa (ko-NEE-chee-WAH)—Japanese
- Privet (preev-YET)—Russian
- M'bolo (mm-BO-lo)—Bulu (Cameroon)

- Hej (hay)—Swedish
- Cooee (koo-EE)—Aboriginal
- Alô (ah-LAW)—Portuguese
- Sabaidi (sub-EYE-dee)—Laotian
- Háo (how)—Sioux (American Indian)
- Namaste (nam-AHS-tee) Hindi

4. Draw pictures or designs to go along with the words. Then sign your name, pop it in the envelope and send it off to a friend!

More Family Fun:

- Learn to say hello in sign language.

- Write to a pen pal. Sometimes in children's magazines they publish letters from kids who want to become pen pals. Check it out!

- Call a friend you haven't seen for a while just to say hi. Or go out of your way to say hello to five (or ten or twenty) people today. It will make them smile!

Holiday Fun

December

Activity Book

December Birthday

Hold court at a royal birthday party. The birthday person is king or queen for the day!

Royal invitations and party decorations

What You'll Need:

- ➤gray construction paper
- ➤brown construction paper
- ➤envelopes
- ➤cone-shaped party hats
- ➤curling ribbon
- ➤aluminum foil or silver spray paint

- ➤posterboard
- ➤construction paper scraps
- ➤markers
- ➤transparent tape
- ➤scissors
- ➤glue

Here's How to Make Them:

1. Invitations: Cut gray construction paper into six-inch squares. For each invitation, cut square notches along the top edge to make a castle tower. Cut a 3" x 4" drawbridge from brown construction paper. Round the top of the bridge. Attach the bridge to the middle of the castle by taping it along the bottom edge only, so it can open and close. Fold the bridge down and write your invitation on the castle piece. (The bridge should cover the words when it is folded up.) Draw stones and windows on the castle with markers. Fold the sides of the castle over the bridge so it will fit into the envelope for mailing.

2. Ladies-in-waiting hats: Cover cone-shaped party hats with aluminum foil or spray paint them silver. Attach long curling ribbons to the tips of the cones. Make one for each girl at your party, or supply the materials and let them make their own.

3. Knight's shield: Cut shields from posterboard and cover them with aluminum foil or spray paint them silver. Glue or tape a handle to the back of the shield. Cut emblems from construction paper and glue them to the front of the shield. Make a shield for each boy at your party, or supply the materials and let them make their own.

4. Birthday crown: Cut a crown from posterboard and cover it with aluminum foil or spray paint it silver. Glue construction paper jewels on the crown. The crown is for the birthday king or queen.

Castle cake

What You'll Need:

➤cake mix
➤9" x 13" pan
➤vanilla cream or fluffy frosting
➤aluminum foil
➤2 chocolate bars
➤toothpicks

➤board, tray, or sturdy cardboard to fit cake
➤miniature marshmallows
➤crepe paper

Here's How to Make It:

1. With a grown-up's help, bake the cake, following the directions on the package for a 9" x 13" single layer. Let the adult remove the cake from the pan to cool completely. Then cut the cake into two pieces measuring 4-1/2" x 9" and one piece measuring 3" x 9". Cut the smaller piece in half crosswise.

2. Transfer one large piece to the foil-covered tray and frost the top. Place the second large piece on top and frost the sides and top of the cake. Then position the two smaller pieces on the outside edges of the cake as towers. Frost them on all sides.

3. Arrange miniature marshmallows all along the top of the cake. Break apart one of the chocolate bars and use the sections for windows. Break off a larger section of the other chocolate bar for a drawbridge. Tape little crepe paper streamers to toothpicks for flags. Stick the flags in at an angle on either side of the drawbridge. Arrange birthday candles on the towers of the castle. Put the completed castle in the middle of your table for a regal centerpiece!

More Party Fun:

Entertain the court with these party games and activities. Choose them according to the ages of your guests.

- Build a castle (All ages) — Stack large boxes and cartons together to make a castle you can climb in, or build smaller versions with building blocks. If you have a sandbox, create sand castles. Or make castles from snow if you live in a cold climate.
- Play "Jester Make Me Laugh" (Ages 3-5 and 6-7) — See page 82 for directions for this game.
- Royal memory game (Ages 3-5 and 6-7) — Use all the face cards from a deck of cards. Shuffle them and lay them face down in a square on the floor or table. Take turns turning over two cards. If the faces match, you keep the cards and continue playing as before. If they don't match, your turn is over. Turn the cards face down again and give the next person a chance. The one with the most matches wins. (To make the game more challenging, use cards from two decks.)
- Slapjack (Ages 6-7 and 8-10) — You can play this card game with up to five people. Shuffle a deck of cards and deal them face down one at a time. (It's okay if some players get more cards than others.) Players cannot look at their cards. Put them face down in a pile in front of you. The birthday person goes first. Take a card off the top of your pile and place it face up in the middle. The next person on the left does the same. Continue in a clockwise circle

until someone turns up a Jack. The first person to slap the Jack gets to add the pile in the middle to his or her stack. Keep playing until one player wins all the cards, or until everyone is tired of playing.

● Royal trivia (Ages 8-10) — Test your guests' nursery rhyme and fairy tale memories with this trivia game. Write the following questions on a large piece of paper. (The answers are at the bottom of the next page—but no fair peeking!)

1. Who liked to bake tarts?
2. Who was a merry old soul?
3. What was the name of Cinderella's fella?
4. Who wore invisible clothes?
5. Who slept on a lumpy mattress?
6. What princess was bigger than her seven best friends?
7. Whose birthday put everybody to sleep?
8. What prince was really good at hopping?
9. What did the pussycat frighten under the Queen's chair?
10. Who had the golden touch?

Post the questions at your party and give each guest a piece of paper and a pencil. Give one point for each correct answer. The person with the most points is the winner.

● Outdoor fun (All ages) — Play "King Midas" tag. The birthday person is King Midas. Players that King Midas tags immediately turn to gold and must remain frozen in that position until another player touches them. The last person King Midas turns to gold becomes the next King Midas.

Answers to trivia game:

1. The Queen of Hearts
2. Old King Cole
3. Prince Charming
4. The Emperor
5. The Princess from *The Princess and the Pea*
6. Snow White
7. Sleeping Beauty's
8. The Frog Prince
9. A mouse
10. King Midas

Nobel Prize Awards Ceremonies
(December 10)

Since 1901, outstanding people from around the world have been recognized for their achievements in physics, chemistry, medicine, economics, literature, and peacemaking. They are given Nobel prizes in ceremonies held in Sweden and Norway.

The prizes are named for Alfred Nobel, a Swedish chemist who, when he died in 1896, left the bulk of his fortune to establish the international awards.

Family "Nobel" awards
(All ages)

What You'll Need:

➤frozen juice can lids (one for each person) ➤permanent fine tip marker

➤ribbon or yarn ➤large nail and hammer

➤gold spray paint (optional)

Here's How to Do It:

1. If you want, spray paint the lids gold on both sides. (Let a grown-up help you with this, and make sure you do it in a well-ventilated area. Cover furniture and rugs with newspaper or drop cloths to protect them.)

2. Let an adult help you punch a hole near the top of each lid by pounding a nail through the lid.

3. Choose categories for the prizes you will award. How about "Best in Washing Dishes" or "Super Reader" or "Top Joke Teller"? Come up with a different category for each member of your family. Write each category on a lid.

4. String yarn or ribbon through the holes in the lids. Then, in a special ceremony, give out the awards to your family. Take pride in a job well done!

Santa Lucia Day
(December 13)

Although Saint Lucia was from Italy, this holiday is uniquely Swedish! Santa Lucia Day marks the beginning of the Christmas season in Sweden. Before dawn on the morning of December 13, the oldest daughter of the house brings breakfast to adult family members still sleeping in bed. Lucia wears a white gown and red sash and on her head is a crown of green boughs topped with lighted candles. Her brothers and sisters accompany her, singing Swedish carols and serving traditional Lucia buns and coffee.

Make a Lucia crown
(Ages 6-7 and 8-10)

What You'll Need:

➤white, green, and red construction paper
➤scissors
➤stapler
➤glue

➤tape
➤orange and yellow markers or crayons

Here's How to Make It:

1. Cut a strip of white construction paper to fit around your head. You may have to staple a couple together to make one long enough.

2. Cut white construction paper into five 2" x 5" pieces. Roll each piece into a cylinder and tape the edge. Cut one end of each cylinder to make a flame shape. Color the flames orange in the middle and yellow on the outside. Staple your candles to the head band.

3. Cut leaves from green construction paper and glue or staple them all around the headband. Cut little berries from red construction paper and glue them in a few places on the headband.

4. Fit the band around your head and staple it together.

Make a star boy hat to accompany Lucia!

(Ages 3-5)

What You'll Need:

➤white poster board

➤star cookie cutter

➤gold foil gift wrap or
  gold foil stick-on stars

➤pencil

➤scissors

➤tape

➤glue

Here's How to Make It:

1. Cut an 18" square of poster board. Draw a curved line from one corner to the opposite corner and cut out along the line. Roll the poster board into a cone shape to fit your head, overlapping the edges slightly. Tape the edges securely.

2. Make gold stars by tracing around the star cookie cutter. Cut out the stars and glue them to the cone. If you have gold star stickers, you can use them instead.

More Family Fun:

● Bake "Lucia Cats," using this easy adaptation of the traditional Lucia bun recipe: Thaw and let rise frozen roll dough you can buy at the supermarket. With clean hands, form each roll into a six-inch snake. Make each snake into a closed-up S shape. Put a raisin in the curves of the S to make the cat's eyes. Place the buns on a greased cookie sheet and bake in a 350° oven for about 15 minutes or until they are golden brown. Serve them on Santa Lucia Day!

● To learn more about the history and traditions of Santa Lucia Day, check out the book, *Lucia: Child of Light*, by Florence Ekstrand. It book is available from Welcome Press, 1095 C Street/Bay View, Mount Vernon, WA 98273.

Posadas
(December 16–24)

In Mexico, the Posadas are nine days of traditional religious celebrations with processions, parades, and elaborate fireworks. Posada (or inn) processions reenact the search of Mary and Joseph for a place to stay in Bethlehem. Two people are chosen to play Mary and Joseph, and they lead a group of friends through the streets, knocking on neighbors' doors and asking to come in. The procession goes from house to house until it reaches a predetermined house where they are admitted. Then the party begins!

Brown bag piñata (All ages)

No posada celebration is complete without a piñata! This one skips the papier mâché step so it is an extra easy one to make for your posada party! (All ages)

What You'll Need:

➤grocery bag

➤construction paper

➤crepe paper in several colors

➤glue

➤strong cord

➤masking tape

➤scissors

➤candies or small treats to put inside

Here's How to Make It:

1. Fill the bag with your candies and treats. Then tie the open end shut tightly. The tied end is the top of your piñata.

2. Cut crepe fringes to fit around the bag. Glue them around the bag in layers, alternating the colors, until the bag is covered.

3. Roll the construction paper into five cones. Tape one cone securely to each side of the bag and one to the bottom. Glue crepe paper around the base of each cone to hide the tape. Glue crepe streamers to the ends of each cone.

4. Hang your piñata by tying a long cord to the top. Throw the cord over a tree branch or other high object. Take turns wearing a blindfold and swinging a stick at the piñata. (Be careful not to stand too close the person with the stick!) When the bag breaks, scramble for the goodies!

More Family Fun:

● Get together other nearby families and host a posada celebra-tion. Walk from house to house, singing songs as you go. At each house, knock on the door and ask if there is room. (At all but the last house, the answer is no!) At the last house, hold a party! Serve Mexican food and play games. Be sure to hang up your piñata!

● If you live in an apartment building, hold your procession in the hallways, go from apartment to apartment. Or, you could hold a family posada party in your home. Just process from room to room until you get to the party room.

Wright Brothers' Day
(December 17)

December 17 marks the anniversary of the first powered airplane flight at Kittyhawk, North Carolina, in 1903.

Build a foam glider (Ages 6-7 and 8-10)

What You'll Need:

- ➤ 11"x 6" (or larger) foam food tray
- ➤ scissors
- ➤ pen
- ➤ large paper clip

Here's How to Make It:

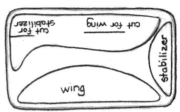

1. Draw the airplane body, wing, and stabilizer on the foam tray as shown here.

2. Cut out the pieces. Cut a slit in the tail section and a slit in the middle for the wing.

3. Insert the stabilizer in the tail and push the wing through the body of the plane. Attach a large paper clip to the nose of the plane and you are ready to fly!

More Family Fun:

● Make a glider for everyone in the family and hold a contest to see who can fly theirs the farthest.

● Which one will go farther—a paper airplane or your foam glider? Try it and see!

● Visit an airport today and watch the planes take off and land. How many planes come and go in a 15 minute period? Check the arrivals and departure board. What is the longest flight posted? Where is it to?

● Play airliner in your living room. Set up chairs in rows to be seats on the plane. Make boarding passes for the passengers. Take turns being the pilot, flight attendant, and passengers. Whoever is the pilot gets to announce where the flight goes.

Hanukkah

The Jewish people have a history that goes back to, well, back to biblical days. This feast celebrates the recovery of the Temple of Jerusalem and its rededication. It is, therefore, a joyous holiday and is marked by many events such as the lighting of candles on the menorah. This commemorates a miracle: oil that burned for eight days, thus, the lighting of a new light on each of eight days. This holiday is also known as the Festival of Lights. It is a time for gift-giving and feasting.

Children are fond of this holiday because much of the observance focuses on games and celebration. The dreidel game is fun. Try it, you'll enjoy it!

Play the dreidel game

(All ages)

What You'll Need:

- ➤cardboard egg carton
- ➤glue
- ➤scissors
- ➤newspaper
- ➤pennies or candies

- ➤two colors of paint
- ➤paint brush
- ➤pencil
- ➤marker

Here's How to Make It:

1. Cover your area with newspaper. Cut off two sections from the egg carton. Paint each a different color. When they are dry, glue the open ends together.

2. Have a grown-up help you stick a sharpened pencil into the top and out through the bottom.

3. Use a marker to write one of the following on each of the four sides of the dreidel: *Nun, Shin, Hay, Gimmel.*

4. To play the game, you need two or more people. Each player gets the same number of pennies or candy. To begin, each person puts one coin or candy in the middle. Take turns spinning the dreidel. If the dreidel lands on Nun, the player gets nothing; Shin, the player puts in a penny or candy; Hay, the player takes half the pennies or candy; Gimmel, the player takes all the pennies or candy. The winner is the person who ends up with all the pennies or candy.

More Family Fun:

● Make and eat potato latkes. Here's a recipe:
Peel and grate 6 medium potatoes and 2 onions. Drain off any extra liquid. Stir in 2 eggs, 4 tablespoons flour, 1 teaspoon salt, 1/2 teaspoon baking powder, and a dash of pepper.
Heat a quarter inch of oil in the bottom of a skillet. Gently place tablespoons of latke batter in the oil. Fry on both sides until golden brown.

Serve your latkes warm with sour cream or applesauce.

National Flashlight Day
(December 21)

This holiday falls on shortest day and longest night of the year. The long hours of darkness on December 21 give you plenty of time to use your flashlight.

Play flashlight tag

(All ages)

What You'll Need:

➤a flashlight

➤a large, dark area

➤at least three people

Here's How to Play:

1. The object of the game is to tag all players using a flashlight's beam, while they try to avoid getting caught. Move fast, but be careful not to bump into anybody in the dark!

2. Give one person the flashlight. That person tries to tag the other players with the beam of light. If you are caught in the beam, you must immediately freeze. You cannot move again unless you are touched by a player who is not yet frozen.

3. The last player caught and "frozen," gets the flashlight, and you start all over again!

More Family Fun

● Shine your flashlight on a blank wall and make shadow pictures with your hands. Can you make a bird or a rabbit or a dog?

● Flashlight Day was invented as a way to brighten up the long dark nights of winter. Plan other ways to brighten up this dark season. Use candles at each family meal. Draw a happy sun picture and hang it in your room. Spend time each evening telling cheerful stories. Designate a day for everyone to wear something yellow. Don't let the dark get you down!

Christmas

(December 25)

Christmas is one of the most joyous fests in the Christian calendar, celebrating the birth day of the Christ Child. Although a religious holiday, it has also become a holiday for remembering those close to us with love and gifts. Gift-giving can get out of hand, and a parent who establishes sensible guidelines for gift-giving is teaching an important value. The mythology that has grown up around Christmas—Santa, Rudolph and the like—make this a magical day for children. Enjoy this family day with love and warmth. Religious in origin, it is also a universal holiday of love. The "spirit of Christmas" is simply that—love for all.

Santa and Rudolph tin lid ornaments (Ages 3-5)

What You'll Need:

- ➤frozen juice can lids
- ➤red felt
- ➤brown construction paper
- ➤black fine tip permanent marker
- ➤hammer and nail

- ➤cotton balls
- ➤red pompom
- ➤craft glue
- ➤ribbon or string
- ➤scissors

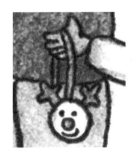

Here's How to Make Them:

1. Have a grown-up punch a hole by driving a nail through the top of each lid. Thread ribbon or string through the hole for a hanger.

2. To make Santa, cut a triangle from red felt and glue it across the top of one lid. Draw on eyes with the marker. Pull a cotton ball apart slightly and glue it to the lower half of the lid and up along the sides for Santa's beard. Glue part of another cotton ball along the bottom edge of the hat and at the tip of the hat.

3. To make Rudolph, cut antlers and ears from brown construction paper. Glue the antlers close to the top on the backside of the lid, so that they stick out on either side. Glue the ears near the top on the front of the lid. Draw on eyes and a mouth. Glue the red pompom to the middle for his "nose that glows!"

Glitter snowflake and star ornaments

(Ages 6-7)

What You'll Need:

➤white craft glue

➤waxed paper

➤pencil

➤glitter

➤plain paper

➤fishing line or thread

Here's How to Make Them:

1. Draw snowflake or star outlines on paper. Place the waxed paper over your drawings and draw over the designs with glue.

2. Sprinkle glitter over the glue. Let the glue dry for at least 48 hours (two whole days!).

3. Carefully peel the waxed paper away from the ornament. Tie on fishing line or thread so you can hang your glitter creations in a window or on your Christmas tree.

Glue together a pretzel wreath ornament

(Ages 8-10)

What You'll Need:

➤12 mini heart-shaped pretzels

➤hot glue gun and glue sticks

➤scissors

➤waxed paper

➤holiday ribbon

Here's How to Do It:

1. Arrange six pretzels in a circle on the waxed paper. Make sure the edges are touching.

2. Let a grown-up glue the pretzels together with hot glue. (Only grown-ups should handle the glue gun!)

3. Make a second wreath like the first. Then glue one wreath on top of the other, matching up the pretzels. Let the glue cool.

4. Starting at the top of the wreath, weave holiday ribbon in and out between the pretzels. Leave a tail of ribbon at the beginning and the end that you can tie in a bow.

5. Hang the wreath on your Christmas tree and make another to give to someone for a gift!

More Family Fun:

● Hold a caroling party! Invite friends over to sing favorite Christmas carols. Walk around your block and share the music of the season with your neighbors, or go caroling at a nursing home or hospital. Go back to your house for hot chocolate and Christmas cookies afterwards.

● Take your family on a shopping trip for a charity that donates toys to kids who otherwise wouldn't get anything for Christmas. Decide how much to spend and then get the nicest toy for your money. Look for toys that won't break easily and are popular with kids. A good rule to follow is buy a toy you wouldn't mind having!

● Writing thank-you notes can be a chore for kids. Make saying thanks more enjoyable by taking snapshots of the recipient wearing the gift or playing with it. Have the photos developed as postcards or pick up special postcard backers at photo developing shops. Then let the kids write a simple thank you on the back. (They don't even have to say what the gift is, because it's pictured on the front!) Address the postcard and zip it in the mail.

Boxing Day
(December 26)

This holiday originated in England. It is a national holiday there and in Canada. On Boxing Day, people traditionally give gifts to the people who work for them or serve them in some way. Give some little boxes of cheer to somebody today!

Fancy boxed gifts (All ages)

What You'll Need:

- small boxes or containers
- tape
- scissors
- markers or crayons
- plain paper
- candy, cookies, or other treat to put in the package

Here's How to Do It:

1. Make a list of people to receive the gifts, such as the mail carrier, trash collector, bus driver, or paper deliverer.

2. Fill each box with treats and stick in a note thanking the person for their help throughout the year. Wrap each box in plain paper.

3. Draw designs on the paper with markers or crayons. Try to make each box reflect the person who will receive it. Make a package for your bus driver look like a bus. Draw letters and postage stamps all over one for your mail carrier or color it like a mail box. Tie a newspaper ribbon to a gift for the person who delivers your paper. A package for your trash collector could be packed in a round container and colored as a little garbage can—but with a pretty bow on top! Use your imagination!

More Family Fun:

● Another way to thank service people is to send their supervisors a letter that praises the job they have done. As a family, write to the bus company, post office, newspaper, or sanitation department. Let them know how much you appreciate their workers. Remember to say thanks to the person, too!

● Long ago, lords used to trade places with their servants on Boxing Day. Try trading places with the grown-ups in your family for one day!

Kwanzaa
(December 26–January 1)

This African-American holiday was created in 1966 to rediscover the rich heritage of African cultural traditions. Kwanzaa means "first fruits," and the holiday is patterned after harvest festivals that still take place in Africa. During the seven days of Kwanzaa, families focus on seven principles: Umoia (unity), Kujichagulia (self-determination), Ujima (collective work and responsibility), Ujamaa (cooperative economics), Nia (purpose), Kuumba (creativity), and Imani (faith).

Weave a mkeka (Ages 6-7 and 8-10)

A mkeka is a mat for the Kwanzaa table. Weave one with the traditional Kwanzaa colors. Black represents the African American people; red stands for their struggle for justice; and green signifies hope for the future.

What You'll Need:

➤red, green, and black construction paper

➤scissors

➤glue

Here's How to Do It:

1. Cut the short side of the red and green paper into strips, about two inches wide.

2. Cut several wavy lines the long way in the black paper. Do not cut all the way to the either edge.

3. Weave a green strip over and under the black paper. Then weave a red strip. Continue alternating the colors. When you are done, glue the strips to the outside edge of the black paper.

Play a counting game with the colors of Kwanzaa

(Ages 3-5)

What You'll Need:

➤ 7 dried lima beans

➤ acrylic paint in red, green, and black

➤ margarine tub with lid

➤ paintbrush

Here's How You Do It:

1. Paint a red dot on one side of three beans. Paint a green dot on one side of three more beans. Paint a black dot on one side of the last bean. Let the paint dry.

2. Put all the beans into the margarine tub and snap on the lid. Give the tub a shake. Take off the lid. How many red beans do you see? How many green? How many black? Count all the beans with their painted side up. Let each person have a turn. The one with the highest number of painted beans wins.

3. If you are older and know more about numbers, you can play the game in a different way. Give each color a value, like one point for red, two points for green, and five points for black. Add up the points for your score.

More Family Fun:

● Visit your library to find and read books about Kwanzaa. A book that describes the celebration with words and photographs is *Celebrating Kwanzaa* by Diane Hoyt-Goldsmith (Holiday House, 1993).

Index of Age Groups

Use this index to locate the activities best suited for your child!

Ages 3-5

Pages 5, 7, 9, 12, 19, 20, 26, 31, 32, 40, 43, 46, 51, 63, 66, 69, 70, 73, 82, 83, 85, 91, 95, 98, 105, 106, 108, 111, 116, 126, 138, 143, 154, 155, 157, 161, 167, 168, 174, 182, 185, 188, 193, 196, 203, 206, 210, 216, 217, 227, 229, 234, 241, 246, 254, 256, 258, 261, 264, 269, 272, 275, 280, 284.

Ages 6-7

Pages 6, 7, 9, 12, 15, 19, 20, 23, 26, 32, 34, 41, 43, 46, 47, 52, 56, 63, 64, 66, 69, 74, 82, 83, 85, 91, 92, 95, 96, 98, 105, 106, 108, 111, 116, 119, 122, 126,138, 140, 154, 155, 157, 160, 161, 167, 168, 170, 173, 182, 183, 185, 189, 193, 197, 203, 204, 207, 210, 213, 217, 218, 221, 227, 228, 229, 231, 234, 238, 242, 246, 254, 256, 258, 260, 264, 266, 269, 272, 276, 280, 283.

Ages 8-9

Pages 6, 7, 9, 15, 19, 23, 26, 32, 34, 41, 43, 47, 48, 52, 56, 63, 64, 66, 69, 75, 82, 83, 86, 92, 95, 96, 98, 105, 106, 114, 119, 133, 126, 130, 138, 140, 154, 155, 157, 160, 161, 168, 170, 173, 182, 183, 185, 189, 197, 203, 204, 207, 213, 218, 221, 228, 229, 231, 234, 238, 246, 254, 255, 256, 258, 260, 264, 266, 269, 272, 277, 280, 283.